Metal Weapons, Tools, and Ornaments of the Teton Dakota Indians

To Marylea Nicholson
With sincere best wishes
James Austin Hanson

Metal Weapons, Tools, and Ornaments of the
Teton Dakota Indians

by James Austin Hanson

UNIVERSITY OF NEBRASKA PRESS • LINCOLN

Copyright © 1975 by the University of Nebraska Press
All Rights Reserved
Manufactured in the United States of America

Library of Congress Cataloging in Publication Data

Hanson, James Austin, 1947–
   Metal weapons, tools, and ornaments of the Teton Dakota Indians.

   Bibliography: p.
   Includes index.
   1. Teton Indians—Implements. 2. Indians of North America—Great Plains—Implements. 3. Teton Indians—Commerce. 4. Indians of North America—Great Plains—Commerce. I. Title.
E99.T34H36   338.4′7′67109701   74–15277
ISBN 0–8032–0849–9

The publication of this book was assisted by a grant from The Andrew W. Mellon Foundation.

*This book, for all sorts of reasons,
is for Charles and Marie.*

contents

List of Illustrations	ix
Preface	xiii
List of Abbreviations for Sources and Credits	xvii
1. Introduction	3
2. Early Trade Goods	11
3. Metal Weapons	14
Firearms	14
Northwest Guns	15
Trade Rifles	20
Breechloading Repeating Rifles	22
Breechloading Single-Shot Rifles	23
Pistols	24
Double-Barreled Shotguns	26
Arrowheads	26
Lance Heads	31
Knife Clubs	35
Tomahawks	38
Swords	45
4. Metal Tools	49
Knives	49
Axes and Hatchets	54
Cooking Utensils	57
Kettles	57
Skillets and Grills	59
Coffee Pots and Cups	60
Leatherworking and Sewing Tools	60
Awls	61
Hide Scrapers	62
Scissors	65
Needles	65
Quill Flatteners	66
Hoes and Spades	67
Firesteels	68
Horse Equipment	68
Files	70
Miscellaneous Metal Tools	70
5. Metal Ornaments	75
Earbobs and Dangles	75
Rings	77
Beads	79
Bells	80
Arm Bands and Bracelets	83
Lead	84
Peace Medals	85
Brass Tacks	90
Pectorals and Crosses	90
Hairplates	93
Belt Disks and Drops	96
Chain and Wire	98
Religious Objects	100
Buttons	104
Miscellaneous German Silver Ornaments	105
Indian Police Uniforms	106
Selected Bibliography	111
Index	115

list of illustrations

1. Ball club (after Carver) — 11
2. Sioux knife (after Carver) — 11
3. Detail of French trade gun, ca. 1700 — 12
4. Side plates from early English trade guns — 12
5. English kettle, ca. 1700 — 12
6. French ax, ca. 1700 — 13
7. French knife, ca. 1700 — 13
8. English knife, ca. 1779 — 13
9. Brass serpent side plate from a Northwest gun — 15
10. Tombstone fox marking on a Northwest gun — 16
11. Fox-in-circle marking on a Northwest gun — 16
12. 1805 Barnett Northwest gun — 17
13. 1831 Jacot Northwest gun — 17
14. Leman Northwest gun, period 1845 — 17
15. Chance Northwest gun, period 1830–60 — 17
16. 1844 Belgian Northwest gun — 19
17. 1870 Barnett Northwest gun — 19
18. J. Henry "New English" rifle — 19
19. Tryon flintlock rifle — 19
20. Leman flintlock rifle — 21
21. Leman percussion rifle — 21
22. Winchester carbine, Model 1866 — 21
23. Winchester owned by Sitting Bull — 21
24. Indian policemen at Standing Rock Reservation — 22
25. .45-70 carbine which belonged to Young-Man-Afraid-of-His-Horse — 23
26. .50-70 rifle made up of parts from military guns — 23
27. Red Dog with Sharps rifle — 24
28. Remington percussion revolver — 24
29. Indian police with Remington revolvers — 25
30. Diamond-shaped arrowhead — 27
31. Arrowhead marked "H. Murphy, Harvard, Mass." — 27
32. Strap iron cut for making arrowhead — 27
33. Barbed war arrowhead — 28
34. Asymmetrical war arrowhead — 28
35. Serrated tang arrowhead — 28
36. Single-notch tang arrowhead — 28
37. Plain tang arrowhead — 28
38. Serrated diamond-point arrowhead — 29
39. Inverted shoulder arrowhead — 29
40. Arrowhead from Custer battlefield — 29
41. Arrowhead from Custer battlefield — 29
42. Blacksmith-made arrowhead — 30
43. Arrowheads found in western Nebraska — 30
44. Buffalo arrowhead — 30
45. Arrowheads from the Upper Missouri — 30
46. Arrowheads from eastern Wyoming — 31
47. Commercial field arrowhead — 31
48. Lance head (after Catlin) — 32
49. Lance head (after Miller) — 32
50. "Assiniboin" lance head found in Nebraska — 32
51. Hafted "Assiniboin" lance — 32
52. Lance head found in western Nebraska — 33
53. Lance head from the Sioux — 33
54. Lance head from Fort Laramie — 33
55. Teton medicine man with lance — 34
56. Lance captured from the Sioux — 35
57. Lance with sheet iron head — 35

#	Title	Page
58.	Gunstock club	36
59.	Transitional knife club from the Yanktons	36
60.	Transitional knife club from the Tetons	36
61.	Early knife club	36
62.	Knife club of Sitting Bull the minor	36
63.	Spotted Eagle, with knife club	37
64.	Straight-handled knife club	38
65.	Knife club from Wounded Knee	38
66.	British pipe tomahawk	39
67.	Pipe tomahawk which belonged to Red Cloud	39
68.	Brule chief Wak-ta-geli, with pipe tomahawk	39
69.	Low Dog, with pipe tomahawk	40
70.	Late plains tomahawk	41
71.	Missouri war ax	42
72.	Missouri war ax	42
73.	Spontoon pipe tomahawk	42
74.	Sans Arc with spontoon tomahawk	43
75.	Poll-hammer tomahawk	43
76.	Good Voiced Crow with cavalry saber	44
77.	Black Horn with sword	44
78.	Indian drawing of Teton swords	45
79.	Indian drawing of mounted warrior with sword	46
80.	Portrait of a Teton with knife sheath, after Carver	49
81.	Teton girl with belt for tacked sheath	50
82.	Furnis knife	50
83.	H. Cutler knife	50
84.	J. Russell knives	51
85.	J. Ward knife	51
86.	Knife stamped "PCJ"	51
87.	J. Russell knife with bolster	52
88.	Wilson spear-point knife	52
89.	Two knives from the Tetons	52
90.	Unmarked knife blade from Wounded Knee battlefield	53
91.	Illegibly marked knife from Wounded Knee battlefield	53
92.	"USID"-marked knife from Wounded Knee battlefield	53
93.	Lamson and Goodnow knife	53
94.	Lamson and Goodnow knife with bolster	53
95.	Large Lamson and Goodnow knife	54
96.	Butcher knife which supposedly belonged to Sitting Bull	54
97.	Large carving knife	54
98.	Hand-forged bowie knife	54
99.	Ax marked "JB"	55
100.	Ax marked "U"	55
101.	Hatchet by I. Blood	55
102.	"George Washington" hatchet	55
103.	Hatchet from the Sioux	56
104.	Collins half-ax	56
105.	U.S. Army scout kettle	57
106.	Dutch oven	58
107.	Sheet iron kettle	58
108.	Brass kettle	59
109.	Short-handled skillet	59
110.	Long-handled skillet	60
111.	Cooking stand or grill	60
112.	Awl with mountain sheep horn handle	61
113.	Straight awl blade	61
114.	Crooked awl blade with deer horn handle	61
115.	Awl made from a knife	62
116.	Awl made from a knife	62
117.	Elk horn scrapers	62
118.	Hide scraper bits and carrying bag	63

119.	Fleshing tool made from a gun barrel	64
120.	Fleshing tool made from square iron rod	64
121.	Tanning tools (scythe blade scraper, dehairing tool, and hand scraper)	64
122.	Small scissors	65
123.	Large shears	65
124.	Nineteenth-century packets of needles (regular and beading)	65
125.	Quill flattener (Oglala)	66
126.	Quill flattener (Brule)	66
127.	Quill flattener (Hunkpapa)	66
128.	Clement and Maynard hoe	67
129.	O. Ames spade	67
130.	Oval firesteel	68
131.	Open-loop style of firesteel	68
132.	Mexican hand-forged bit from the Oglalas	68
133.	1862 army issue McClellan saddle	69
134.	McClellan saddle from the Custer battle	70
135.	Collection of miscellaneous items from the Wounded Knee battlefield	71
136.	Silver trade ornaments	76
137.	Brass earbob	76
138.	Beaded pouch with tin cone dangles	77
139.	Ring made of lead	78
140.	Brass ring	78
141.	German silver ring	78
142.	A hank of cut steel beads	79
143.	Brass beads and chain	79
144.	Photograph of Short Bull showing the use of brass beads	80
145.	1800 period cast brass bell	81
146.	Cast brass bell with copper rivet for attachment	81
147.	Heavy nineteenth-century cast brass bell	81
148.	Large iron bells, period 1880	81
149.	Brass hawk bells	82
150.	Two Oglalas with bells on costumes	82
151.	Narrow factory-made German silver arm bands	83
152.	Complete bracelet or arm band from Wounded Knee battlefield	83
153.	Fragment of bracelet from Wounded Knee battlefield	84
154.	Fragment of arm band from Wounded Knee battlefield	84
155.	Lead-inlaid pipe	85
156.	Teton wearing British peace medal	86
157.	Reverse of Jefferson peace medal	87
158.	Reverse of Andrew Johnson peace medal	87
159.	Pierre Chouteau, Jr., Company trader's medal	88
160.	Obverse of Washington trader's medal	88
161.	Reverse of Washington trader's medal	88
162.	Tetons wearing stamped brass medals	89
163.	Brass-tacked knife sheath from Wounded Knee battlefield	90
164.	Pectoral from the Oglalas	91
165.	Pectoral worn by White Eyes	91
166.	Aberrant form of pectoral	91
167.	Oglala wearing cross	92
168.	Nickel-plated brass cross from an Oglala	93
169.	Miller's painting of Fort Laramie showing the wearing of hairplates	94
170.	Hairplate set	95
171.	Running Water and family, in 1868, showing the two styles of hairplates	95
172.	Brule wearing hairplates	96
173.	Set of miniature hairplates	96
174.	Teton woman wearing conch belt	97

175. Belt with German silver disks — 97
176. Belt disk from Wounded Knee battlefield — 98
177. Teton with brass loop earrings — 98
178. Brass wire bracelets — 99
179. Teton woman wearing brass wire bracelets — 99
180. Obverse of Catholic Immaculate Conception medal — 100
181. Reverse of Catholic medal — 100
182. Pewter crucifix — 101
183. Long Dog wearing a crucifix — 102
184. Crucifix worn by Sitting Bull — 102
185. Episcopal Niobrara cross — 102
186. Lieutenant Bullhead wearing Niobrara cross — 103
187. Small brass crucifix — 103
188. Obverse of DeSmet medal — 104
189. Reverse of DeSmet medal — 104
190. Buttons from an Oglala campsite near Fort Robinson, Nebraska — 104
191. White Thunder wearing German silver breastplate — 105
192. German silver awl case — 105
193. Hunkpapa German silver bridle — 106
194. Indian Police uniform coat and belt — 107
195. Early Miller's 101 Ranch Show badge — 107
196. Later Miller's 101 Ranch Show badge, worn by Bear Shield — 108
197. Crossed-arrows Indian scout helmet ornament — 108

Preface

This book is intended as both a guide to the identification of typical Teton metal objects and when and how they were used, and a study in the transition of the Teton Sioux Indians from a stone age people in the eighteenth century to a nation almost totally dependent by 1880 on white man's goods obtained from traders and through other channels.

Metal objects were important to the Tetons. They replaced many of the prehistoric tools and weapons and added greatly to the Indian's ability to decorate himself and his possessions. They increased his productivity and created leisure time. Since metal was the most durable of the goods the Tetons obtained from the whites other than the ubiquitous bead, and thus is a fairly reliable index of their intercourse with white men, a study of the metal objects which they used in the prereservation period offers a valuable insight into Teton culture and acculturation. After 1880, the regular sources of metal through trading and warfare were gone, and the Teton found himself totally dependent upon the reservation storekeeper and government blacksmith for his metal goods.

The fur trader who served as middleman in this commerce between white man and Indian was a businessman with an unorthodox clientele. He sought to maintain peace on the frontier, for war invariably slowed trade. Contrary to some reports, he did not haul junk five hundred or a thousand miles. Popular myths and even noted historians have led many to believe that the

Indians traded away their valuable pelts for cheap and gaudy merchandise of low quality. The trader provided sturdy utensils which filled the Indians' needs; only when these needs were filled did he bring out the gaudy ornaments and whiskey to win the Indians' remaining furs. Most traders knew that the Indians must have good tools to live well and produce the furs that made both white and red man prosperous. The metal tools and weapons obtained by the Tetons were generally well made and of a practical nature—well adapted to the strenuous and mobile life of the Tetons. The Tetons never demanded more nor accepted less. As for the ornaments, the German silver and brass hairplates, conch belts, and crosses were no more ostentatious than the full-trail war bonnets, buffalo horn headdresses, and painted robes that the Indians made before the advent of trade goods.

In selecting specimens for inclusion in this study, I have used objects which were obtained by the Tetons from trading companies and federal peace commissions, as annuity goods, and in warfare. Objects acquired by unusual means or from peculiar sources are usually not included. Indians obtained unique items—lodge regalia, clocks, padlocks, canes, and compasses, for example—from travelers, explorers, and army troopers, but they were never basic parts of Teton material culture. The range of this class of artifact is limited only by the technology of the times.

Museum pieces from the Tetons are scarce because many of the items have lost their identity through years of storage or improper labeling. The only appreciable archaeological studies of nineteenth-century Teton culture have been done through surface finds at battlefields and campsites. The Tetons followed a nomadic life over such a large area that major archaeological finds have been confined essentially to the sites of trading posts in areas controlled by the Tetons.

Because Indians modified commercially produced items and even manufactured items themselves, unscrupulous dealers have been making fake items for sale as genuine Indian objects. I have generally used only objects obtained directly from the Tetons or from noted and reputable collections. Many items can be found in museums and collections which are "believed to be Sioux," but none of these were used in this study. Only when no examples of items known to have been used by the Tetons could be found were specimens from neighboring tribes included.

This work originated as a master's thesis at Chadron State College, Chadron, Nebraska, in 1970. Credit for the initial concept goes to William M. Beauchamp, who in the first decade of the twentieth century wrote *Metallic Tools of the New York Indians* and *Metallic Ornaments of the New York Indians*. Although both of these books are antiquarian in approach and much of the information is now outdated or has been found to be erroneous, many people have considered them to be invaluable.

The research for this book has been continuous. I have examined well over ten thousand objects to determine typical Teton metal objects of the nineteenth century. A considerable part of my research in Washington, D.C., was financed through a grant from the Smithsonian Institution, for which I am most grateful. Further study in England was made possible by a grant under the National Museum Act, administered by the Smithsonian Institution. My research there included the Plains Indian collections of the major English museums and commercial data pertaining to the fur trade in libraries and archives.

In addition, a great number of individuals have contributed to this book. With no desire to offend any of those not mentioned here who rendered assistance, I wish to acknowledge my debt to the following persons who have made significant contributions. Mrs. Jackie Wilson assisted with manuscript preparation. Dr. Kenneth O. Leonard, president, Museum Association of the American Frontier, helped in locating objects for inclusion in the study. The staffs of the Missouri Historical Society and the National Archives were of invaluable assistance in locating needed documents and records. Dr. John C. Ewers and others of the Smithsonian Institution gave generously of their time. Charles E. Hanson, Jr., editor, the *Museum of the Fur Trade Quarterly*, gave freely of his time and patience in reading and criticizing the text. These people bear no responsibility for errors and omissions which may appear. They are mine alone.

Canyon, Texas   J. A. H.

Abbreviations for sources and credits

DPL	Denver Public Library Western Collection, Denver, Colorado
HDC	Bill Hudson–Frank Dodd Collection, Crawford, Nebraska
KOL	Kenneth O. Leonard Collection, Garrison, North Dakota
MAI	Museum of the American Indian / Heye Foundation, New York, N.Y.
MFT	Museum of the Fur Trade, Chadron, Nebraska
MHS	Montana Historical Society, Helena, Montana
NARS	National Archives and Records Service, Washington, D.C.
NPS	National Park Service, Moose, Wyoming
SI	Smithsonian Institution, Washington, D.C.

Metal Weapons, Tools, and Ornaments of the Teton Dakota Indians

Chapter One

Introduction

The enormous transformation from a stone age to a modern culture which the Teton Sioux underwent in two centuries following their first contact with the white man can be attributed in large degree either directly or indirectly to the influence of the fur traders. When the French, then in sole control of the northern fur trade, first heard of them in 1640, the Sioux inhabited the country west of Lake Superior on the headwaters of the Mississippi. Although they called themselves *Dakota*, from *koda*, the Siouan term for "friend" or "ally," the name by which they are most commonly known comes from the Chippewa word *Nadowe-is-iu*, "adder" or "snake," and by extension, "enemy." Since the early French explorers were in closer contact with the Algonquin Indians, of whom the Chippewas were a branch, they adopted a variant of the Chippewa term, *Nadowessioux*, for the Dakotas.

The Dakotas comprised three main divisions, each of which spoke a different dialect. The eastern group, or Santee Sioux, which spoke Dakota, encompassed the Sissetons, Wahpetons, Wahpekutes, and Mdewakantons. Exhibiting the Woodland culture traits, they remained east of the Mississippi and were designated on early French maps as Sioux of the East. The middle, or Wiciyela, division consisted of the Yanktons and Yanktonais, who spoke Nakota. Along with the western, or Teton, division, they ranged across the prairies east of the Mississippi and were known as the Sioux of the West. They displayed characteristics of both the Santee and the Teton culture. The Tetons, who spoke Lakota, took their name from the term *Titonwan*, "Dwellers of the Prairie." Evidently this group originally comprised a single tribe but ultimately it fragmented into seven. The Tetons underwent the transition to nomadic buffalo hunters at an early date: two of the first white men to live among the Sioux, Recollet missionary Father Louis Hennepin in 1680 and French entrepreneur Pierre Charles Le Sueur in 1700, both commented that the Tetons were unlike their eastern tribesmen. Hennepin wrote: "They do not use canoes, nor cultivate the earth, nor gather wild rice. They remain in their skin houses, generally in the prairies which are between the Upper Mississippi and the Missouri Rivers, and live entirely by the chase."[1] Thus at the time of first white contact the Tetons were following a pattern of life which was not greatly changed but rather greatly facilitated by the acquisition of the horse and metal objects.

After 1660 the Tetons had begun a migration southward into the Minnesota Valley, later turning west. The full explanation for this movement is open to debate, but pressure from their enemies, the Chippewas and Crees (who were both supplied with guns by French traders after 1650 and by the English operating out of Hudson Bay after 1670) certainly had much to do with it. The Yanktonais, who lived nearest the Crees, were probably affected most dramatically. One of their subtribes, the Assiniboins, broke off completely and allied themselves with the Crees (the Dakotas called the Assiniboins *Hohe*, meaning "rebels"). Perhaps the Tetons also wished to escape the domination of the Eastern Sioux, who were closer to the traders, and they may have migrated in search of buffalo herds as well. Their acquisition of large numbers of horses during the later migration period, between 1730 and 1760, facilitated their movement greatly. (I am inclined to accept the later date because the Tetons were then near the Arikaras, who served as middlemen in trading horses from the south and west.)

Before 1700 the Tetons divided into two groups, the northern, or Saone, whose name died out by the middle of the nineteenth century, and the southern, comprising the Oglalas and Brules. Not yet a very powerful people, the Tetons turned west, the southern group reaching the Missouri River first, about 1760, near the Big Bend. Their migration was spotty, and they did not settle there but continued to range back into Minnesota. The southern Tetons split at the Missouri, and the Oglalas, some mounted, some afoot, crossed it first and continued to move west, reaching the Black Hills about 1775. They settled along the Bad River of present South Dakota and were in undisputed control of the region by 1790. The Brules followed the Oglalas a little later, moving down the White River Valley south of the Bad River, and by 1810 were located on its headwaters. The Saones arrived north of the Big Bend of the Missouri about 1790. There they divided, one part going northwest and crossing the Grand River before 1830, the other pushing southwestward to settle north of the Oglalas. In these migrations the Tetons displaced the Iowas and Otos, and later the Arikaras, Cheyennes, Arapahos, and Crows.

Each of the Saone groups split, the northern into the Hunkpapas and Siasapas (Blackfoot Sioux), the southern into the Miniconjous, Itazipcos (Sans Arcs), and Ooenonpas (Two Kettles). The seven Teton tribes were lined up on a north-south axis from the Platte River to the Heart River.

Early in the nineteenth century, then, the Tetons were in the locations where they would become well known to white Americans and where they would have their reservations. They roamed from the Missouri to the Rockies until forced onto reservations in the 1870s. The Oglalas pushed west and south against the Cheyennes, Kiowas, Arapahos, Shoshonis, and Crows. They drove the Kiowas far south, pushed the Shoshonis and Crows against the east slope of the Rockies, and allied themselves with the Cheyennes and Arapahos. The Brules raided the Pawnees on their southern boundary and the Missouri River tribes to the east. While the Saones fought the Blackfeet with little effect, they did great damage to the Upper Missouri tribes, and continued in league with the Yanktons against the Crees and Chippewas.

Trade was a well-established practice among the Indians long before the coming of the white man; there was an appreciable amount of trade between the prehistoric peoples of America. Archaeologists have recovered catlinite beads and pipes a thousand miles from the stone's source, and sea shells from both coasts frequently turn up in archaeological excavations deep in the interior of the continent. Unlike modern commerce, however, this trade was incidental to survival and was not essential to the maintenance of culture.

The permanent villages of the Missouri—those of the Mandans, Hidatsas, and Arikaras—served as focal points for a prehistoric trade in meat and robes, which were brought in from the plains on either side to exchange for cultivated crops. John Ewers delineates a so-called protohistoric, or transitional, trade pattern, a development from the earlier intertribal trade, in which the traditional objects of commerce—products of the chase or of cultivation—were replaced by introduced articles of white manufacture acquired from the still far-distant white man.[2] While the trade among Indians in native products by no means ended in the historic period, it was overshadowed by the predominant flow of commerce.

The protohistoric trade patterns were determined largely by the sources of supply and the demand for the primary items of barter—horses and metal trade goods, particularly firearms. Horses were plentiful in the Spanish Southwest, and enterprising Mexicans and Christian Indians found a good market for ponies and horse gear among the nomadic tribes of the southern plains, who in turn dispersed them northward. At the same time that the horse was revolutionizing the life of the Plains Indian—beginning in the latter half of the seventeenth century—firearms were spreading westward from the Mississippi and Great Lakes traders. The permanent villages of the Missouri were ideally located for exchange points, and the Arikaras and Mandans acted as middlemen in passing horses from the southern and southwestern tribes to those farther east and north, and guns in the opposite direction. The Dakotas had their own trade center, located east of the Missouri along the James River in present Minnesota, which was used into the nineteenth century. The eastern Dakotas brought trade goods from white posts along the Minnesota River, while the Tetons brought items from the Arikaras on the Missouri. The Tetons also occasionally went directly to the traders at the Minnesota River. Pierre Antoine Tabeau, a trader to the Arikaras who was present at the annual trade fair of the Dakotas about 1803, noted that firearms, kettles, catlinite pipes, and walnut bows were sought by the Tetons, who purchased them with horses, buffalo robes, and leather goods.[3]

Perhaps as early as 1630 the Dakotas saw metal which had come from the East Coast through slow tribe-to-tribe routes. Most Indian tribes were familiar with native copper and some had seen gold and silver. Metal also filtered up from the Spanish settlements in the Southwest, but iron was scarce there until the nineteenth century. Small metal objects like knives, awls, and firesteels probably preceded firearms in the protohistoric trade. A gun is of questionable usefulness when one must depend upon an erratic aboriginal commerce for powder and lead. Moreover, a dozen small iron tools were much more easily transported than an extra gun with a supply of powder and bullets for it.

Traders made their way onto the plains remarkably early, and their trade goods changed the balance of power wherever they went. Traders operating out of Canada reached the Sioux before 1700, but the bulk of their commerce was with the Sioux' enemies. There is little wonder that in the 1690s a Sioux chief made the fatiguing and dangerous trip to Montreal to beg for trade goods. He saw clearly the bleak future of the Dakotas should they be unable to neutralize the effect of their enemies' superior weapons. He told the governor of New France, Frontenac, "All the nations have a father who protects them. All have iron weapons; pity me, for I have none."[4] As Le Sueur traveled up the Mississippi in 1700 he encountered Canadian traders, indicating that a significant fur trade commerce had already developed along that great water artery. On arriving at the villages of the Sioux of the East, he remarked that they were "the masters of the other Sioux . . . because they are the first with whom we traded, which has given them a good supply of guns." The Frenchman recorded the entreaties of one Sioux leader: "Behold thy children . . . ; it is for thee to see whether thou wishest them to live or die. They will live if thou givest them powder and ball; on the contrary, they will die if thou refuse it." One wonders whether the Sioux were in fact as destitute as they seemed or if the speeches were part of the game Indians and traders played for three hundred years. In any event, Le Sueur did dispense some goods to the Dakotas including fifty pounds of powder, fifty pounds of bullets, six guns, ten hatchets, and a steel calumet.[5]

The French were dominant in the trade around the headwaters of the Mississippi until they relinquished ownership of Louisiana to the Spanish in 1763, but the English had been active competitors since the establishment of the Hudson's Bay Company in 1670. A Teton winter count for 1705–1706 records that the Tetons made the long trip to Hudson Bay and purchased a quantity of kettles from the English post.[6] If they did, they probably bought other trade goods as well. After the transfer of Louisiana, the English began to take over the northern trade. The Northwest (or North West) Company, organized in 1783–84 with headquarters at Montreal, as a competitor of Hudson's Bay, was the chief British firm dealing with the Indians on the Upper Mississippi until the merger of the two firms under the name of the older one in 1821. The Michilimackinac Company, which was established toward the end of the eighteenth century and operated from Mackinac Island (also known as Michilimackinac), was evidently a leader in the British invasion of Spanish Louisiana, with traders reaching as far as the Yanktons and Tetons.[7]

The Spanish, although seldom able to maintain themselves against the English, did well in trying to hold the Mississippi Valley. They had trouble with the Sioux, however. A Spanish militia officer named Malliet scouted the frontier around Saint Louis during the Revolutionary War. He found the Sioux to be pro-English, not caring especially for the French or Spanish, and in 1778 a trader named Lucas David, licensed by the Spanish, was murdered by the Sioux. The Spanish had issued presents to the Dakotas in Ylinueses (Illinois, the district of Spanish Louisiana that included Saint Louis) in 1770, and two thousand pounds of goods were sent to the Sioux the same year by a trader who reported that they were peaceful and business was quite good. He distributed Spanish medals to the chiefs.[8]

Several English traders, in 1786, reported that the Dakotas were so numerous and scattered that no one could accurately estimate their strength.

> They occupy the plains on the east side of the Mississippi . . . and are esteemed War like and fierce but not very good hunters [for furs] owing to their Country being stocked with Buffaloe and the little intercourse they have with the Traders (of late however they are become more industrious, and the best Deerskins with a deal of Beaver and Otters are now obtained from them.[9]

In 1787, English traders passed out coats and flags to Dakota chiefs, among whom was at least one Teton.[10] The Anglo-Dakota friendship continued into the nineteenth century. Sioux Indians, probably of the eastern group, had taken part in an abortive assault on Saint Louis in the Revolutionary War, and Dakota warriors were allied with the British in the War of 1812.

After the British became entrenched in present Minnesota, the French traders, under Spanish license, began successfully to penetrate the Upper Missouri, to which point the Tetons had removed. Regis Loisel, who has been tentatively identified as either the Good White Man or Little Beaver of the Teton winter counts, brought a good supply of firearms to the Tetons in the 1790s.[11] Hugh Héné traded with the Oglalas and Saones, and Tabeau with the Brules, in the period 1800–1805.[12] Lewis and Clark noted several traders traveling to or from the Teton villages, so that it is safe to say that by 1804 there was a regularly established, if small, commerce between the Tetons and the traders from Saint Louis.

The Tetons used their increasing power to make their influence felt. Attempts of French traders to reach the Mandans in the late eighteenth century yielded little but trouble, and Jacques d'Eglise, a trader who successfully made the trek in 1790, noted that perpetual war existed between that tribe and the Dakotas.[13] Tabeau remarked that the Tetons were bullies to an exceeding degree, making life miserable for the Missouri River tribes.[14] There is little reason to doubt that in very early days the intertribal trade on the Missouri was an important vehicle in acculturation, but once the Tetons had other sources for goods, they used earlier friendships as excuses to bully the Arikaras and steal their horses. It was in large part due to Teton persecutions that the Arikaras moved upriver in the early nineteenth century to escape their tormentors.[15] Tabeau commented that the Arikaras traded frequently with the Sioux. The Arikaras were very poor traders, usually overpaying for what they received. They failed, in Tabeau's estimation, to comprehend any sense of business or profit making.[16]

The Tetons gradually dissolved their trade connections with the Northwesters in the Minnesota region and established relations with the traders of the Missouri. The Spanish authorities, who had at least tried to open the fur trade in this area, bowed out with the sale of Louisiana to the United States. Saint Louis would grow as America's gateway to the fur fields, and English competition for the Teton trade would virtually end by the 1820s.

The early trade, however, must not have been too important. Pike wrote in 1805 that the Mdewakantons, Sissetons, and Yanktons were trading at Michilimackinac, and that the Sissetons and Yanktons supplied the "Yanctongs of the north, and Titongs, with the small quantities of iron works which they require. Fire arms are not in much estimation with them." Pike further noted that the Tetons numbered eleven thousand souls, but owned only a hundred guns. The Yanktons numbered 4,300, with 350 guns, and the 2,160 Sissetons possessed 260 guns. Each of the 2,049 Chippewa warriors owned a firearm.[17]

Tabeau made some very perceptive comments as to the reasons for the lack of trade with the Tetons. He observed that the nomadic people followed the buffalo, rather than hunting or trapping the fur-bearing small game. The Indians who hunted buffalo on horseback with bow and arrow disliked the exertions of trapping. They cared little for the trade goods of the white man, having little real need for them.[18]

Tabeau was quite correct in his assertions. Until about 1840, the beaver dominated the fur trade. The early western fur trade was directed toward the Rocky Mountains and white trappers usually gathered the pelts. By 1820, the mountain man trade had initiated heavy commercial traffic on the Missouri River. However, the Plains tribes did almost no trapping, and so the only items the traders sought from the Tetons were deerskins for leather and a few buffalo hides. The Tetons could muster enough skins to purchase basic needs, but articles of decoration and fancy metal goods were scarce before 1835.

With the gradual decline in the value of beaver pelts caused by changes in fashion and the acceptance of the silk hat, the emphasis on the Rocky Mountain fur trade diminished. About the same time, settlers began pouring into Iowa, Illinois, and Minnesota. The demand for buffalo hides from these settlers for carriage robes and coats brought a shift of the trading companies' efforts to the plains. Buffalo robes, which the Tetons had had in excess since the acquisition of the horse, became prime currency. The Tetons were able to satisfy their hunger for trade goods, and more and better weapons made them more powerful. Objects which had been unknown and unneeded in prehistoric times were now necessities which no smartly dressed, well-equipped Teton could be without. Major depots were constructed by the trading companies all around the Teton country so that by 1840 the Tetons were never more than a few days' ride from a trader. Ironically, the settlers, the very people who created the market which made the Tetons wealthy, were the ones who would eventually press Congress to open Teton lands for settlement.

The development of the Upper Missouri trade was in many ways the result of continued efforts to oust the British from the area. In 1808, two famous fur companies took form. Manuel Lisa, a highly successful and competitive trader, established the Missouri Fur Company in Saint Louis and John Jacob Astor obtained a charter for the New York-based American Fur Company. By 1817, Astor had absorbed virtually all the American posts of the Northwest Company and the assets of the old Michilimackinac Company, which had been temporarily reorganized as the Southwest Company.

The Saint Louis traders could not prevent the American Fur Company from expanding its efficient and powerful operations into their territory. In 1822, Astor established in Saint Louis the Western Department of the American Fur Company. The Missouri Fur Company went out of existence in 1830, and General William Ashley's unorthodox and brilliant effort to compete for beaver pelts, the Rocky Mountain Fur Company, lasted from 1822 to 1834.

Competition from another area was taking shape. British traders on the prairies who found themselves south of the international boundary after the War of 1812 established the Columbia Fur Company in 1821 as an American firm. Finally, in 1827, this company united with the American Fur Company as the Upper Missouri Outfit.

Astor saw greater profits in other fields, and went out of the fur business in 1834. The eastern departments of the American Fur Company continued under that name, while the Saint Louis–based Western Department was purchased by Pratte, Chouteau and Company, a cooperative firm controlled in the main by distinguished fur traders of French descent. Four years later, in 1838, the firm became Pierre Chouteau, Jr., and Company.

Two major fur trade centers and a minor one grew up in Teton country. In present-day central South Dakota, a series of posts—Forts Lookout, George, Defiance, Tecumseh, and Pierre—were built, abandoned, and rebuilt. The most important of these was Fort Pierre. It was the eastern terminus of the traders' road to the second major center in present eastern Wyoming. There the traders established Forts William, John (commonly called Fort Laramie), Bernard, Platte, and several smaller houses. Fort Laramie emerged as the principal trading post, but the Chouteau firm abandoned it in 1849 and reestablished the western depot near modern Scottsbluff, Nebraska, naming it Fort John.

The minor trade center (minor not because of its volume but because of its only occasional use by the northern Tetons) was on the Missouri's Big Bend. These were Forts Lisa, William, Clark, Berthold, and Union. Fort Union evolved as the main trading post and depot in this area.

As always, there were confident and daring men willing to offer a little competition to the major company. To the southwest, Bent and St. Vrain dominated the trade in present-day Colorado. On the Platte River, Lancaster Lupton made serious inroads into the trade, while the Sybille and Adams Company cut Chouteau profits in the Black Hills. On the Upper Missouri, a New York firm, Fox, Livingston and Company, tried and failed to establish itself in the trade. Troublesome competition also arose sporadically from Robert Campbell, United States Indian superintendent, who quietly helped to organize a series of trading companies operating on the Missouri.

Through it all, the financial strength and operating efficiency of Pierre Chouteau, Jr., and Company enabled the great firm to watch, if nervously, the competition come and go. As was the case with the American Fur Company, the Chouteaus' large trading posts served as supply depots for hundreds of company traders and even independents who operated one- or two-man wintering posts or who visited outlying camps with wagons loaded with merchandise.

The trading companies carried on a lively business with the Tetons. It reached mammoth proportions in the 1840s and provided the Tetons with easy access to literally tons of goods which greatly simplified their life. The Tetons reached their maximum strength in the late 1850s and dominated the plains from the Rockies to the Missouri River, and from the Platte River to the Canadian border. The Teton domain was strategically placed, for almost every major road to the West either ran directly through their lands or was within easy reach of their highly mobile war parties. Moreover, the Tetons were a connecting link between the Southwest, Great Lakes, and Canadian plains trading areas. In one year, Teton warriors might fight the Blackfeet, who traded with the Hudson's Bay Company, the Kiowas, whose goods came primarily from the Mexicans, and the Chippewas, who were supplied by the Lake traders. Thus the Tetons might possess Woodland weapons such as ball clubs, Hudson's Bay Company dags, and Spanish pectorals at the same time.

From the 1850s to 1877, the friction between the Tetons and nontrading whites erupted into a sporadic, disruptive, and costly war. The Chouteau leaders knew that trade would be erratic, and profits would be more sure and perhaps even greater in other endeavors. The Civil War also upset the other end of the fur business, so Pierre Chouteau, Jr., and Company sold out in the 1860s, most of the trading assets going to the Northwestern Fur Company, headquartered in Saint Paul, Minnesota. One other firm, Durfee and Peck of Leavenworth, Kansas, made a last bid for the trade. The former company closed in 1877; the latter in 1876.

The high-risk trade during the Indian Wars, the coming of rail transportation, and government controls on the sale of certain types of weapons to Indians allowed the independent trader to stage a real comeback in the post–Civil War period. Generally these traders were former Chouteau men, married to Indians, or their mixed-blood children.

The trade with the Tetons ended because of their defeat by the army and their removal to reservations. Coincident with this was the destruction of the bison herds by professional hide hunters, which completely undercut the Teton culture as well as the fur trade. The federal government virtually never interfered directly with the fur trade, but indirectly destroyed it as a major frontier business by the enforcement of its Indian policy.

The federal government also contributed in several ways to the Tetons' material culture. As a part of all treaty negotiations, the federal agents issued presents to various leaders. However, these gifts were generally contracted from regular trading companies, transported by the contracting firm, and frequently issued to the Indians by the company traders. The same is true of the annuity goods issued as payment for land cessions to the government in this period. The companies apparently liked the arrangement, making a guaranteed profit on the goods and increasing their prestige among the Tetons as the distribution medium. Lewis and Clark gave out presents in 1804, and the first treaty payments to the Tetons were in 1825. By the 1850s the government had added huge amounts of food and clothing, two items seldom stocked in large quantity by the traders, to the annuity goods that were issued. The annuity payments caused friction within the government during the Indian Wars, for one branch of the government, the Bureau of Indian Affairs, was supplying the Tetons with arms and ammunition "for hunting," at the same time the army was endeavoring to force the Tetons onto reservations.

In 1866, the Commissioner of Indian Affairs forbade the sale of fixed ammunition or weapons which used cartridges to hostile Indians. The order was apparently impossible to enforce in such a large region as the West, but at least an attempt was made to regulate the trade. This was the only regulation on trade goods, other than a total ban on the sale of liquor.

The army, in its frequent clashes with the Tetons, unwillingly contributed the latest in military weapons, saddles, and other useful equipment to the Indian arsenals. The Indians, too, lost guns to the soldiers, so there was probably no net gain in the numbers of firearms owned by them. The new weapons also introduced increased problems in obtaining proper ammunition, but the army guns were much superior to the muzzleloaders many Tetons carried.

Finally, with the demise of the fur trade on the plains, the federal government could enforce its authority over the Tetons at will. By 1880, the traditional annuity goods were completely replaced by agricultural tools, sad irons, shoes, wagons, sewing machines, and the like. The government turned from making friends with the Indians to making farmers out of them.

Notes

1. Quoted in Doane Robinson, *A History of the Dakota or Sioux Indians* (Minneapolis: Ross and Haines, 1955), p. 29.
2. John C. Ewers, *Indian Life on the Upper Missouri* (Norman: University of Oklahoma Press, 1968), pp. 14–33.
3. Annie Heloise Abel, ed., *Tabeau's Narrative of Loisel's Expedition to the Upper Missouri* (Norman: University of Oklahoma Press, 1939), pp. 122–23.
4. Rev. Samuel William Pond, "The Dakotas or Sioux in Minnesota as They Were in 1834," *Minnesota Historical Society Collections* 12 (1908): 355–56.
5. R. G. Thwaites, ed., "1700: Le Sueur's Voyage up the Mississippi," *Collections of the State Historical Society of Wisconsin* 16 (1902): 186–87, 191, 192.
6. Garrick Mallery, "Picture Writing of the North American Indians," *Tenth Annual Report of the Bureau of American Ethnology, 1888–1889* (Washington: G.P.O., 1893), p. 295.
7. Lawrence F. Kinnaird, ed., *Spain in the Mississippi Valley, 1765–1794*, 3 vols. (Washington: G.P.O., 1949), 3: 439.
8. Ibid., 2: 414, 318, 235–36.
9. R. G. Thwaites, ed., "Memoranda Relative to the Indian Trade," *Collections of the State Historical Society of Wisconsin* 12 (1892): 81.
10. Ibid., p. 89.
11. Mallery, "Picture Writing," p. 313.
12. Abel, *Tabeau's Narrative*, pp. 25–27.
13. Kinnaird, *Spain in the Mississippi Valley*, 4: 93–94.
14. Abel, *Tabeau's Narrative*, pp. 131–32.
15. George Hyde, *Red Cloud's Folk: A History of the Oglala Sioux* (Norman: University of Oklahoma Press, 1937), p. 25.
16. Abel, *Tabeau's Narrative*, pp. 145, 151.
17. Zebulon Montgomery Pike, *Sources of the Mississippi and the Western Louisiana Territory* (Ann Arbor, Mich.: University Microfilms, 1966), Appendix to Pt. 1, pp. 62, 66–67.
18. Abel, *Tabeau's Narrative*, pp. 162–64.

Chapter Two

Early Trade Goods

figure 1. Carved wooden ball club with steel blade, after Carver.

figure 2. Eighteenth-century Sioux knife, after Carver.

Our knowledge of the Tetons and the trade goods they used before Lewis and Clark is sketchy. Archaeologists have as yet uncovered little from this early period in what was then the very far western frontier. Indeed, we know little enough about the colonial fur trade in the East, where it was of such immense proportions and importance in the struggle for a continent. In colonial times, French items were less numerous and more expensive than those of the Dutch, and later, the English, but the *coureur de bois*, the French distribution medium, went farther afield than the English trader. The latter was all too prone to remain at his post and wait for his customers to come in.

Goods known to have reached the Tetons before Lewis and Clark include long guns, knives, hatchets, kettles, lead, peace medals, brass wire, pistols, iron for arrowheads, lances, and bells.[1] In addition, small items like firesteels, awls, and silver ornaments probably enjoyed wide usage before the nineteenth century.

One of the few early travelers to illustrate his narrative was Jonathan Carver, who visited the upper Mississippi country in the 1760s. He reported that there were some firearms among the Sioux, but remarked that the standard weapon was the bow and arrow. Some Indians carried spears with bone points. The typical hand weapon of the Indians was the ball club which had a blade affixed to the ball. This blade, "like a hatchet," was made of iron or flint, "whichever could be procured."[2] The ball club remained a popular weapon among the Woodland tribes. The sedentary tribes and the tribes on the forest fringes seem to have used the "gunstock" club, while the nomadic Tetons preferred the knife club. However, in the middle eighteenth century, the ball club, with or without a spike or blade in the business end of the weapon, was surely the typical Teton hand-held fighting tool. The ball club sketched by Carver is depicted in figure 1.

Carver noted that there was one type of knife peculiar to the Sioux. It closely resembles, in his drawing, the plug bayonet used by military forces in the seventeenth and early eighteenth centuries. It is also similar in some respects to the nineteenth-century "dag," or stabber knife, sold by the Hudson's Bay and Northwest companies, and supplied to nearly all the Canadian Indians and Eskimos. According to Carver, however, these were found among the Sioux only, and were originally made of flint or bone. With the availability of steel from traders they were now made of metal. These knives were "about ten inches [long] and that part close to the handle nearly three inches [wide]. Its edges are keen, and it gradually tapers to a point." These were carried in a sheath and hung around the neck. "This curious weapon is worn by a few of the principal chiefs alone, and considered both as a useful instrument, and an ornamental badge of superiority" (figure 2).[3]

The firearms which the Tetons received from Le Sueur

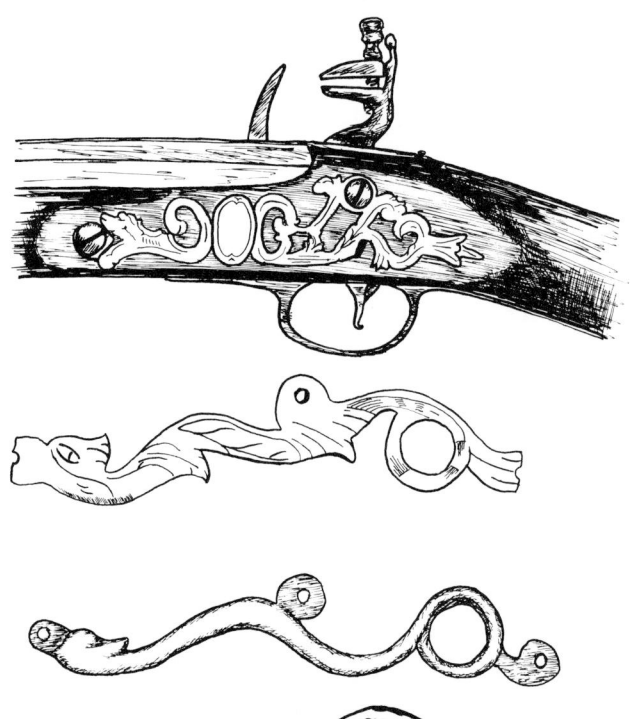

figure 3. French trade gun, showing the brass side plate with oval "mirror" section, period 1680–1720. (MFT)

figure 4. Two brass side plates from early English trade guns. At the top is the flat, engraved style, ca. 1750–70. The bottom specimen is a smooth casting, ca. 1720–50. (MFT)

figure 5. English kettle with flat sheet brass ears, ca. 1700. (MFT)

and other French traders were probably of the type from which a detail is shown in figure 3. Four complete specimens and forty fragments of specimens of this kind of gun have been noted by T. M. Hamilton, virtually all of them found in the Mississippi Basin, and no examples have yet been unearthed in areas of early Dutch or English occupation.[4] It is the most common early French trade gun. This "mirror-sideplate style" trade gun was generally brass mounted, with an engraved small-bowed trigger guard and a side plate with an oval medallion, or "mirror," in the center and a fanciful monster's head at the front. It was a very light-caliber gun for the period, with a bore of about .50 and a barrel three to four feet long. Other types of French guns probably also reached the Dakotas (for the range of possibilities, see Hamilton's *Early Indian Trade Guns*).

English guns that the Dakotas probably received after the French and Indian War were very much like the standard Northwest gun, which is discussed later. The major variations of early English guns from the Northwest gun are the small brass trigger guard instead of the large iron-loop trigger guard used later, and the snake side plate which is either flat and engraved by hand or cast, with an absence of scales, rather than the fancy serpent which is commonly associated with the regular Northwest gun. Two early side plates are shown in figure 4. By 1771, and probably earlier, the Northwest gun had been developed as the standard type of firearm supplied to the Indian.

The kettles which Teton winter counts mention as obtained from the English at Hudson's Bay in 1705–1706 were probably of the type shown in figure 5. Beaten copper or brass kettles with spherical bottoms are occasionally encountered in Indian sites of the middle seventeenth century. By the 1680s most of the kettles were shaped much like those sold in the nineteenth century. Most of these early kettles have flaring sides with a very heavy rim and are relatively shallow. They appear to have been made by spinning, but it is probable that hammering was also used in forming them. Covered kettles are not common before the French and Indian War. The early kettles bought by the Tetons probably differed from the later style only in the form of the ears. Instead of being cast, the earlier ear was either a folded sheet or a folded strip. The folded sheet-brass ear was riveted to the kettle, with a hole near the top through which the bail passed. The strip ear was simply a piece of brass bent twice to form an inverted U which was then riveted to the rim of the kettle.

There does not seem to be much specific information about other early trade goods. A typical hatchet of the period 1680–1720 is shown in figure 6. The French, or "Biscay," ax generally had a greater slope to the eye than did those of England or the Netherlands. One difference between colonial trade axes and those of the nineteenth century is that the earlier type has, when viewed from the top, straight, tapering sides, and the later type has a thinner blade and a more gradual taper that bulges out around the eye.

A typical French knife of the late seventeenth century is depicted in figure 7. This specimen is from an Iroquois site. It has a long, tapered point, and has had a riveted handle. The name on the blade is "ANTOINE DUCHON." An English knife from a 1779 Iroquois site is shown in figure 8. It also has a riveted handle, which is of bone.

The steel calumet mentioned by Le Sueur might have been a pipe tomahawk, or more probably, a steel pipe like those encountered occasionally in colonial sites. These pipes closely resemble the clay pipe of the period. Pewter and silver examples, usually with longer stems, are fairly common.

Other early trade goods mentioned—arrowheads, lance heads, brass wire, bells, silver ornaments, awls, firesteels, and medals—are discussed later in the text.

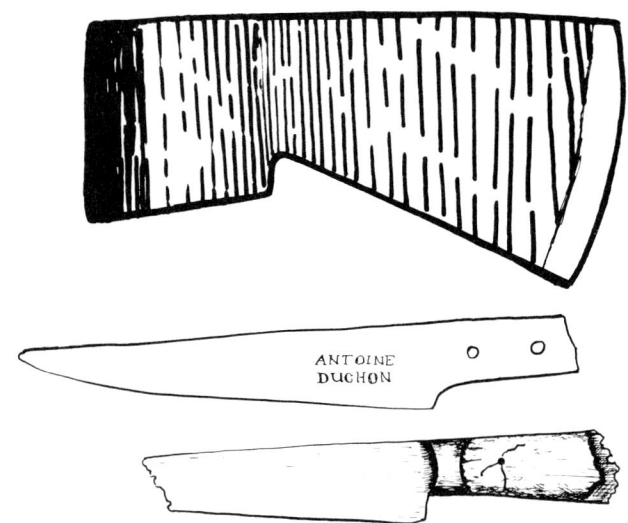

figure 6. French ax with sloping eye, period 1680–1720. (MFT)

*figure 7. French knife blade, ca. 1700, which originally had a riveted handle marked "*ANTOINE DUCHON*." (MFT)*

figure 8. English knife with bolster, from an Iroquois village destroyed in 1779. (MFT)

Notes
1. Abel, *Tabeau's Narrative*, pp. 170–71.
2. Jonathan Carver, *Travels through the Interior Parts of North America* (Minneapolis: Ross and Haines, 1956), pp. 295–96.
3. Ibid., pp. 296–97.
4. T. M. Hamilton, *Early Indian Trade Guns* (Lawton, Okla.: Museum of the Great Plains, 1968), pp. 6–9.

Chapter Three

Metal Weapons

The Sioux were most interested, at least before 1840, in iron, which was superior to flint or bone in weapon making. The Dakota word for iron is *maza*. A trader is called *mazopiye wicasa*, from *maza; opiye*, "a cache," or "a place where things are put away"; and *wicasa*, "man." A trader, then, is an "iron cache man." Firearms are *maza wakan*, or "holy iron." Silver or money is called *maza ska*, "white iron." Iron was the principal metal wanted; as rapidly as they could, the Indians replaced lithic blades with those of iron. The only prehistoric weapon which survived the coming of the iron age was the long and deadly granite-headed war club. For this, the trader could supply no suitable substitute.

The iron weapons were sometimes fashioned by the Indians, using tools bought from traders, but most were commercially produced. A good many were also fabricated at large trading posts, virtually all of which had a blacksmith. A traveler named E. De Girardin noted that Fort Pierre in 1849 had a shop making all sorts of iron goods. The posts regularly ordered tools, both for sale and their own use. Large quantities of sheet, bar, strap, and rod iron of different qualities were on hand at each post.[1] Lewis and Clark's smith did a heavy business in making goods as far back as 1804.

The smiths also were repairmen for the Indians. As an example of the volume of work done, in one year the two blacksmiths at St. Peters Indian Agency (Eastern Sioux) in Minnesota made 4,545 pieces; shod 61 horses; and repaired 1,227 guns, 774 traps, and 546 axes. The items which they made were mostly traps, axes, hoes, muskrat spears, and fish spears. The grand total for the two men was 7,757 articles made, repaired, or mended.[2]

Firearms

Guns were among the first major items received in trade by the Tetons. Le Sueur brought guns to the Dakotas in 1700 and evidently other traders were already supplying them. According to the Teton winter counts, the first guns in any number were traded to them sometime between 1799 and 1802. This imprecision in dating may be explained in two ways: the winter counts of the various bands often differ in reporting the time of specific occurrences by as much as three years, and there is also the possibility that each of the separate tribes of the Tetons got firearms in quantity at different times because of their varying geographic positions.[3]

By 1804, the Tetons were well acquainted with guns and other metal weapons. When Lewis and Clark visited the Brules on their way up the Missouri River in 1804, they found those Indians menacing and unfriendly, possibly because the expedition was proceeding upstream to visit the Mandans, enemies of the Tetons. Sergeant Ordway, one of the explorers, commented that "about 200 Indians were on the bank. Some had firearms, some had spears. Some had a kind of cutlashes [sic] and all the rest had bows and steel or Iron pointed arrows." Clark reinforces Ordway's statement with the remark that the Brules "had their bows Strung & guns Cocked."[4]

Zebulon Pike also observed the early existence of firearms among the Tetons. He estimated in 1805 that the Teton warriors numbered about two thousand and owned approximately one hundred guns. While Lewis and Clark met traders on the Missouri, Pike noted that the Tetons received their trade goods from Mackinac via the Yanktons to the east.[5] All indications point to the fact that the early Teton firearms seen by Lewis and Clark were sold to them by English traders from the Northwest Company's posts around the Great Lakes.

Northwest Guns

The term "Northwest gun" was applied to the whole class of typical firearms sold by all the fur-trading companies, both American and Canadian. Northwest guns were made to a standard pattern from about the middle of the eighteenth century to the beginning of the twentieth century. It is a light smoothbore fusil stocked to the muzzle. The original barrel length varied from twenty-seven to forty-eight inches. The barrels are octagonal for about seven inches at the breech, then the octagon becomes round or sixteen-sided for three to four inches and the remainder of the barrel is round. There is generally only a low blade front sight and no rear sight. The caliber varies from .50 to .70 of an inch. The stock furniture (butt plate, side plate, and rod guides) is brass. The butt plate is flat and quite wide, and the the side plate is cast in the form of a dragon or sea serpent (figure 9). The trigger guard is a large iron loop, so made to facilitate shooting while wearing

figure 9. Detail of the brass dragon or sea serpent side plate which is characteristic of Northwest guns made for the Indian trade. The large iron guard is also typical of these weapons. Two English proof marks and the barrel maker's initials, TB (for Thomas Barnett), are on the barrel near the breech. (MFT)

figure 10. *Detail of 1831 W. Jacot gun lock. The tombstone fox mark is seen just in front of the hammer. Below the fox are the letters "IA," believed to stand for J. J. Astor, and put on the gun in imitation of Hudson's Bay and Northwest Company maker's and inspector's initials. (MFT)*

figure 11. *Detail of 1844 "Burnette" lock showing fox-in-circle mark. The letters "IA," just visible within the circle and beneath the fox, are thought to stand for J. J. Astor's initials. (MFT)*

mittens. These fusils are stamped on the lock, barrel, and stock with a variety of marks. The maker's name frequently appears on lock and barrel. The date of manufacture, if given, is invariably on the lock. Proof or inspection marks are stamped on the barrel. Many Northwest guns bear trading company inspector's marks on the lock, barrel, and stock. These company marks were of two basic designs in the nineteenth century, a fox in a rectangle, or a fox in a circle (figures 10 and 11).[6]

A Barnett Northwest gun is shown in figure 12. This is a Northwest Company gun, manufactured in England for sale to Indians. Charles Hanson feels that it is typical of the early Northwest guns purchased by the Tetons. The lock is marked "BARNETT / 1805" and the barrel is stamped with two English proof marks and "TB" for "Thomas Barnett." The gun has a flint lock and a forty-eight-inch barrel. In addition, this specimen has some early features. The barrel does not have the sixteen-sided segment but rather is round, and the butt plate is nailed on with five square nails instead of being affixed with screws. A fox in a rectangle with the letters "EB" is stamped on the lock. The guns purchased by the Tetons were probably shorter than this specimen to facilitate their use on horseback.

As the nineteenth century progressed, American traders brought firearms up the Missouri River. The American Fur

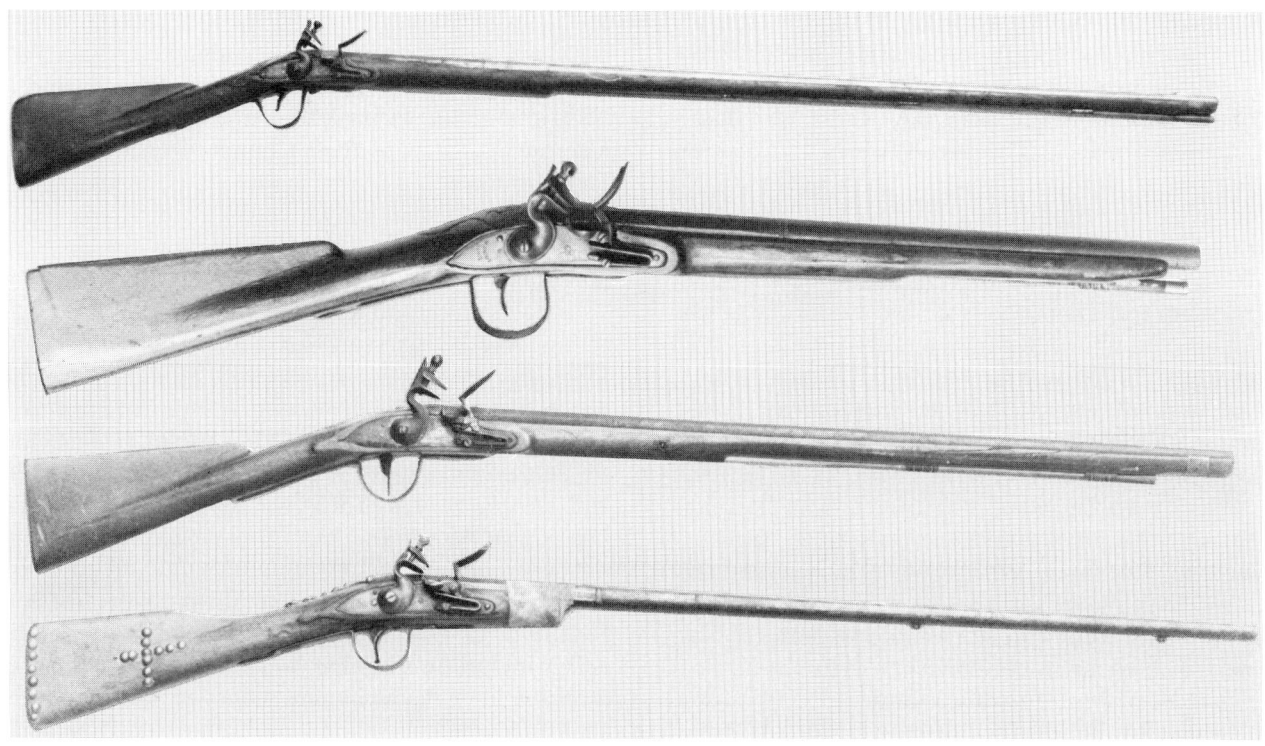

figure 12. English-made Northwest gun by Barnett, dated 1805. The forty-eight-inch barrel is original and probably longer than those supplied to the Tetons. This is believed to be the type in use by the Tetons when they were visited by Lewis and Clark. (MFT)

figure 13. English-made Northwest gun by W. Jacot, who was actually a merchant selling firearms to the American Fur Company. Barrel has been shortened for use on horseback. (MFT)

figure 14. American-made Northwest gun by Henry Leman, Lancaster, Pennsylvania. The thirty-six-inch barrel is original length. Guns by this maker were supplied by some traders to the Tetons, and thousands were given out as payments under various treaties. (MFT)

figure 15. English-made Northwest gun by William Chance, period 1830–60. The barrel length is original, but the wood fore end has been cut off and the stock repaired with rawhide. The butt shows brass tack ornamentation. This and the Belgian trade gun in figure 16 were the most common Northwest guns among the Tetons. (MFT)

Company sold Northwest guns by a variety of makers, notably Jacot and Lacy. Figure 13 shows a sawed-off Jacot Northwest gun dated 1831. A fox in a rectangle, or, as Hanson has named it, a "tombstone fox," with the letters "IA" for "John Jacob Astor," is stamped on the lock. The barrel carries the customary proof marks and is stamped "LONDON." The letters "TB" on the barrel refer to Thomas Barnett, from whom Jacot probably acquired his barrels. The barrel has been cut to nineteen inches by an Indian to increase its usefulness on horseback.

Of the American makers of the Northwest guns, none was more prolific in providing guns for the Teton traders than Henry Leman. Leman's factory in Lancaster, Pennsylvania, turned out thousands of guns for traders and for the United States government's annuity issue programs.[7] A Leman Northwest gun is shown in figure 14. It is marked with "H. E. Leman" and a tombstone fox on the lock and barrel. The barrel is marked with fake British proof marks and is stamped "H.E.L." and "Lancaster Pa." The barrel is thirty-four inches long and is .70 caliber. The overall length of the gun is forty-nine inches. The butt plate is affixed with two screws, a late feature. This weapon is generally heavier in construction than the typical English or Belgian Northwest gun of the same period.

Northwest guns by W. Chance, a maker for the Pierre Chouteau, Jr., Company, were used by the Tetons and at least one was captured from them.[8] One specimen (fig. 15) in the Museum of the Fur Trade at Chadron, Nebraska, shows obvious Indian usage. The forestock has been cut off three inches in front of the lock and a rawhide band has been shrunk around the barrel and remaining forestock. The lock is marked "W. CHANCE & SON" with a tombstone fox. The barrel is stamped "LONDON" with British proof marks. The overall length of this flintlock is forty-nine and one-half inches. The barrel is thirty-three inches long. The existing records from the Pierre Chouteau, Jr., Company, which operated both Forts Pierre and Laramie, indicate that that company purchased a minimum of 2,780 Northwest guns from William Chance and Son between 1850 and 1855.[9] It is certain that the American Fur Company also purchased guns from Chance. In the course of this study, I encountered only ten Chance guns, including detached barrels and locks; this may give the reader some idea of both the rate of destruction of durable trade goods and the number of specimens still to be found.

Belgian manufacturers turned out a large number of cheap Northwest guns for the plains trade. The Chouteau Company sold many fusils made in cottage factories around Liège. Records indicate that the Belgian guns, while cheap in price, were poor in quality. One trader at Fort Laramie wrote to Saint Louis in 1850: "The Belgian Guns sent heretofore will answer very well if it was not for the Lock, and we must beg of you, to try and have them with better Locks—or we do not want them at all."[10]

Specimens of Belgian Northwest guns are fairly common. It is notable that the Belgians copied British guns almost exactly, including marking locks and barrels with British proof marks and makers' names. Some of these spurious markings are "Sargant," "Burnett," and "Burnette" instead of "Sargent Bros." and "Barnett," the names of two noted English gun makers. Figure 16 shows a Belgian Northwest gun marked "BURNETT" over "1844" on the lock. The barrel is marked "LONDON" and "E.B." Both British and Belgian proofs are stamped on the barrel, and the lock and barrel are stamped with a fox and "IA" in a circle. The barrel is thirty-six inches long and the total length of the gun is fifty-two inches. The Chouteau Company purchased guns like this from the 1830s through the 1850s.[11]

A Hudson's Bay Company Northwest gun by Barnett (fig.

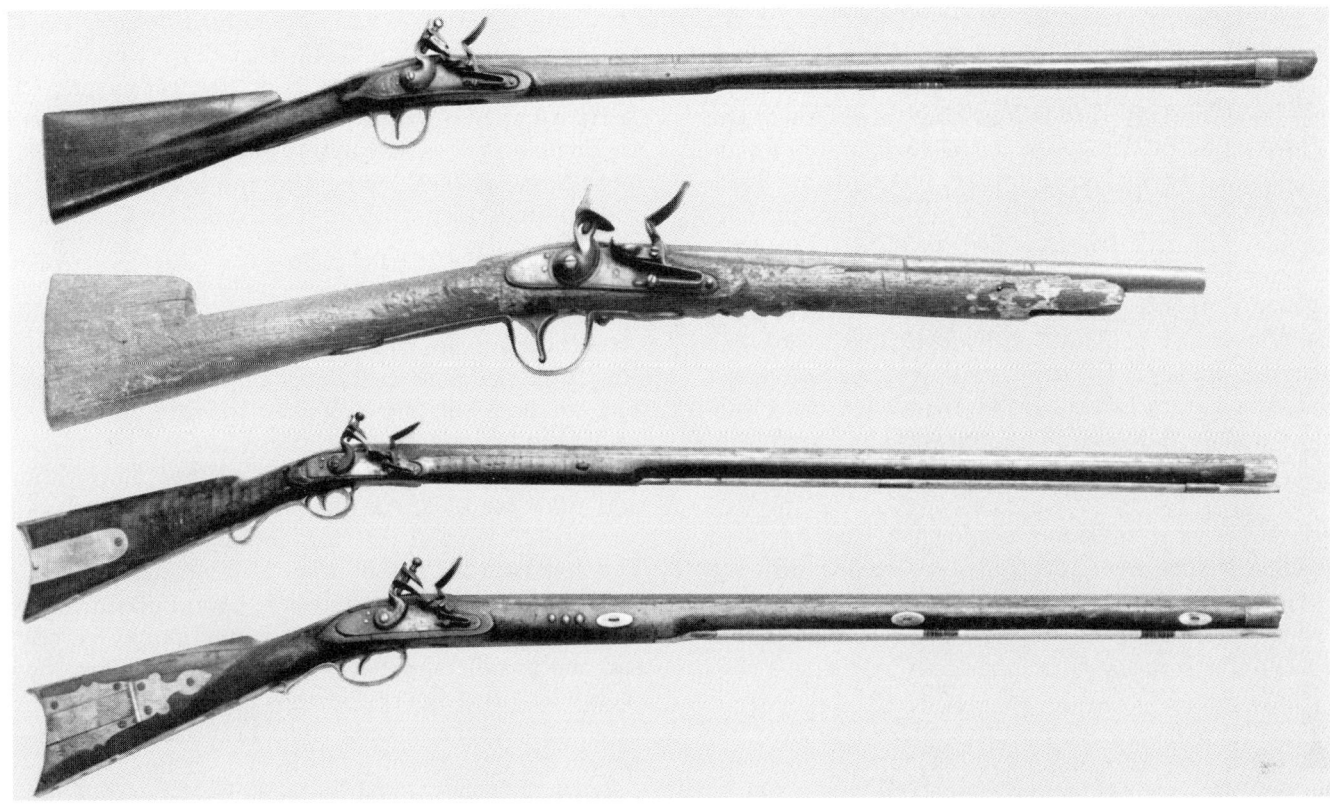

figure 16. *Belgian-made Northwest gun dated 1844 with spurious English marking* "BURNETTE" *on the lock. This is the type sold in large quantities by the Chouteau Company. (MFT)*

figure 17. *English-made Northwest gun by Barnett, dated 1870. The barrel has been shortened and the comb of the stock has been cut away by its Indian user. Found on the bank of the Yellowstone River in Montana. (MFT)*

figure 18. *Indian rifle made by J. Henry, Boulton, Pennsylvania. This is the "New English" pattern, quite popular among the Tetons in the period 1830–55. (MFT)*

figure 19. *The Indian rifle made by Edward K. Tryon, Philadelphia, Pennsylvania, period 1835–50. Large brass patch box on the butt, silver barrel key escutcheons, and checkered wrist were common factory decorations. The brass tacks were added by the Indian owner. (MFT)*

17) was found on the Yellowstone River about thirty miles from Crow Agency, Montana. The top jaw of the hammer is gone and the hammer screw is broken. Presumably it was thrown away by retreating Tetons following the Battle of the Little Big Horn in 1876. The gun is dated 1870, and has been extensively reworked by its Indian owner. The comb, or cheek rest, has been cut down, the butt plate is missing, and the barrel has been sawed off to a length of twenty inches. This may have been brought to the Sioux by the Métis, or mixed-blood traders of Canada. It is typical of the "buffalo runner" guns used by the Plains tribes. The Smithsonian Institution has another specimen made by the same manufacturer and dated 1876. It was taken from Sitting Bull's band when they surrendered at Fort Buford in 1881. This gun was purchased from the Hudson's Bay Company while the hostiles were in exile in Canada.

Two other American makers are known to have supplied small quantities of Northwest guns to whites dealing with the Tetons. They are Tryon of Philadelphia, period 1850, and J. Henry, whose shops were at Boulton, Pennsylvania, period 1850.[12]

Trade Rifles

As the Tetons' desire for more and better trade goods increased, the traders began shipping them large quantities of flintlock and percussion rifles. While these rifles were often double the weight of a Northwest gun, their value was greatly enhanced by the deadly accuracy with which the rifle fires bullets when compared to the hundred-yard-range of the average Northwest gun. My brother, using a Leman percussion rifle of the type made for the Teton trade, fired at and struck a twelve-inch plate twelve consecutive times at two hundred yards. Thus the range and accuracy with which these rifles could be used for long-distance shooting necessary on the plains undoubtedly accounts for their popularity among the Tetons.

Between 1836 and 1841, the Pierre Chouteau, Jr., Company ordered at least 525 "New English pattern" rifles from J. Henry of Boulton, Pennsylvania.[13] One of these rifles with an English-style patch box is depicted in figure 18. The barrel is forty-six inches long and the overall length is fifty-two and one-half inches. Both the barrel and lock are stamped "J. Henry."

Orders by the Chouteau Company also went to Edward K. Tryon of Philadelphia. In 1850, the Chouteaus ordered "100 Indian Rifles."[14] A specimen of Tryon's "Indian Rifle" is illustrated in figure 19. The lock is stamped "TRYON-PHILADA." The barrel is thirty-two inches and the gun forty-six inches long. It is a flintlock.

Henry E. Leman also manufactured flintlock and percussion rifles for both the fur traders and government annuity payments.[15] Two of his rifles are shown in figures 20 and 21. The first (fig. 20) is a flintlock and is characteristic of the period 1850. It is a cheap flintlock, plain but sturdily made, and stamped "H. E. LEMAN" over "LANCASTER PA." on both the lock and the barrel. The barrel is thirty-six inches long and the overall length of the specimen is fifty-one inches.

The second specimen (fig. 21) is marked in the same manner as the one shown in figure 20. It has a percussion lock, however, and was probably made in the period 1860–70. The barrel is thirty inches long and the total length of the gun is forty-five inches. It shows several rawhide repairs at the wrist, lock, and forearm. Of 160 muzzleloading firearms captured from the Tetons and Cheyennes in 1877, 94 were percussion Leman rifles. This specimen is one of those.[16]

Other muzzleloading rifles were also used by the Tetons. Also captured in 1877 were six rifles by S. Hawken of St. Louis, three by J. Golcher of Lancaster, Pennsylvania, fourteen United States Army muskets of unknown type, and

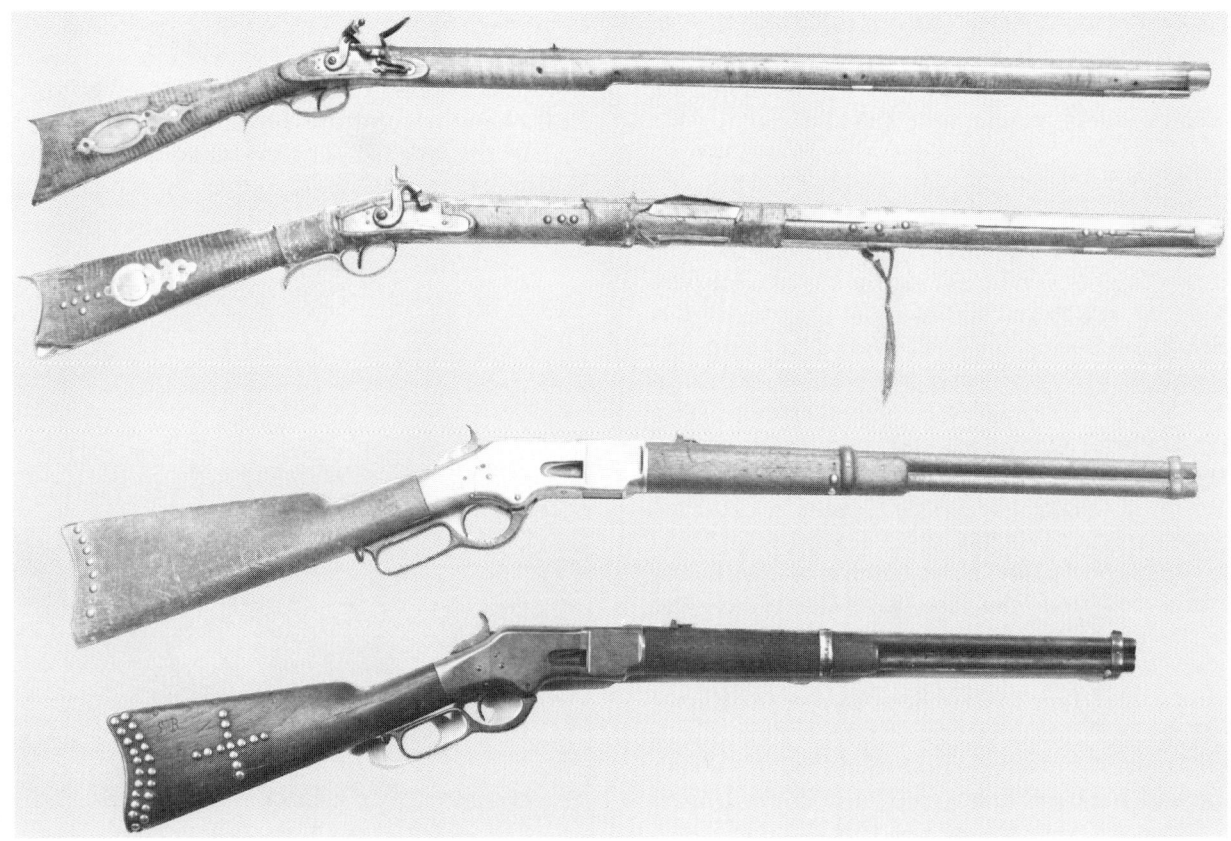

figure 20. Flintlock rifle made by Henry Leman, Lancaster, Pennsylvania. These were sold by traders and given to Indians by the government peace commissions. (MFT)

figure 21. Leman percussion rifle showing extensive rawhide repairs and brass tack decorations. This specimen was surrendered by the hostile Tetons about 1877. These were given out by the United States government in the period 1850–70 in fulfillment of treaty obligations. (MFT)

figure 22. Winchester Model 1866 carbine, caliber .44. Brass tack decorations indicate Indian usage. This specimen was made in 1875 and could have been used at the Custer battle. This was a favorite weapon sold by itinerant traders after the Civil War. (MFT)

figure 23. Winchester Model 1866 carbine surrendered by Sitting Bull in 1881. (SI)

four British muskets of the Enfield pattern.[17] By the time of the Indian Wars, regular trade channels were disrupted, and the Indians were using all sorts of firearms which came from new sources—dead soldiers, immigrants, and settlers.

Breechloading Repeating Rifles

The first repeating rifle used by the Tetons was probably the Henry fourteen-shot .44 caliber rifle brought out in 1862. The Henry rifle saw limited service among the Tetons, for only about 10,000 were manufactured and many of them were purchased for military use during the Civil War. The Henry led to the development of the Winchester Model 1866, shown in figure 22. About 200,000 of these were manufactured before 1880, and many of them found their way into Teton camps. Major Reno, testifying about the Custer battle at his court-martial in 1879, stated that all the hostile Indians he observed in the battle were carrying Winchesters.[18] Doubtlessly, Reno exaggerated to help his own cause, but a number of Winchester carbines were captured from the Tetons.[19] The Winchester shown in figure 22 has extensive Indian decorations of brass tacks on the stock and is in the serial number range of those manufactured and sold in time to have been used in the Custer battle. Figure 23 is the Winchester Model 1866 carbine which was Sitting Bull's personal firearm. He surrendered it through his son when he and his band finally returned to the United States in 1881.[20] It is not known if he had this gun during the turbulent year of 1876, but in any event, it deserves recognition at least as great as that accorded Cornwallis's sword of Yorktown fame. Its surrender was a general's last gesture in admitting his defeat and retaining his pride as an officer and a gentleman.

One other type of breechloading repeater enjoyed some popularity among the Tetons. About seventy-five Spencer carbines were captured by the Tetons at the Fetterman battle in 1866. Several army seven-shot Spencers were later captured from the Tetons. Two were surrendered by the part of Sitting Bull's band who returned to the United States in 1881.[21]

In the late 1870s many Indian police were equipped with Whitney-Kennedy lever-action rifles (fig. 24). Most are

figure 24. Two Indian policemen at Standing Rock Agency, late nineteenth century. Both are carrying Whitney-Kennedy rifles and Remington cartridge revolvers. (DPL)

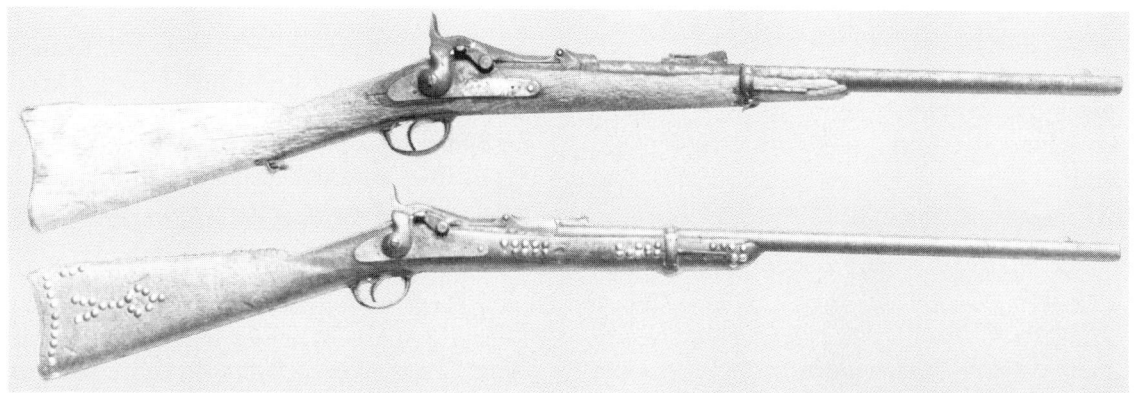

figure 25. *United States Springfield cavalry carbine, Model 1873, caliber .45–70. The serial number (15004) places it in the range of those captured from Custer's men in 1876 at the Battle of the Little Big Horn. It was owned by Young-Man-Afraid-of-His-Horse. (MFT)*

figure 26. *Composite rifle made from a United States Army Model 1866 .50–70 barrel and receiver and a .45–70 stock and lock. This gun was captured by troops from Fort Robinson, Nebraska, sometime between 1879 and 1890. (MFT)*

marked "USID" for the Department of the Interior. A number of Model 1877 Remington-Keene bolt-action carbines were also issued and are similarly marked. One of these from the Oglalas was studied; it had an arrow one inch long engraved on the barrel midway between the receiver and rear sight. "USID" was stamped on the left side of the receiver.

Breechloading Single-Shot Rifles

United States Army rifles after 1866 were single-shot breechloaders in .50 and, later, .45 caliber. A number of them were captured from soldiers. Over two hundred Springfield .45–70 carbines were captured at the Battle of the Little Bighorn. Other rifles and carbines were captured in smaller numbers at other engagements. These weapons were extremely accurate. Testimony indicates that sharpshooters with the .45–70 carbine could deliver deadly fire at ranges up to six hundred yards.[22]

Figure 25 depicts a .45–70 carbine which was owned by the Oglala chief Young-Man-Afraid-of-His-Horse. It is regulation issue Model 1873 except that the saddle ring has been sawed off the left side of the stock. The gun is forty-one inches long and has a twenty-one-inch barrel. The lock plate is stamped with an eagle and "SPRINGFIELD" over "1873." The top of the receiver is stamped with an eagle head, crossed arrows, "1873," and "P" for "proved." Another army gun from the Tetons is shown in figure 26. The barrel and receiver is from a .50–70 rifle. It shows evidence of having been burned. The stock is from a late .45–70 carbine. It was surrendered at Fort Robinson, Nebraska, about 1890.

Other breechloaders were used by the Tetons in the post–Civil War period. Christian Sharps made single-shot breechloading rifles which were captured in some quantity from Tetons.[23] A Sharps rifle can be seen in figure 27, a photograph of the Oglala warrior Red Dog.

Occasionally, various models of Civil War carbines turn up which may be from the Tetons. These were probably captured from volunteer cavalry units. The most common (three examples) of these from the Tetons is the Gallagher carbine.

Pistols

There was little reason for the Tetons to purchase the flint or percussion pistols which were common before the Civil War. Those carried by most white men were hardly as accurate as the Indian's bow and arrow, and certainly less accurate than a sawed-off Northwest gun. Tabeau did remark, however, that the Brule who guarded his post was armed with a pistol.[24] The fur companies purchased flint pistols for their traders and some of these may have been sold to Indians. These were usually long-barreled, plain, and brass mounted, with smooth bores.

Following the Civil War, the traders began selling hundreds of war-surplus Remington and Colt percussion revolvers. These pistols, firing six shots without reloading, became favorite rapid-fire horseback weapons. A Remington percussion revolver from the Oglalas is shown in figure 28. Traders at

figure 27. *Red Dog with a heavy Sharps buffalo rifle. Note the curious cartridge holder at his side. (SI)*

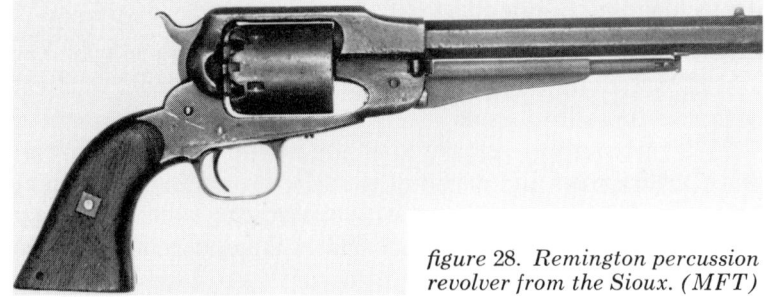

figure 28. *Remington percussion revolver from the Sioux. (MFT)*

figure 29. *Two Indian police with Model 1875 Remington revolvers. The one on the left is using a stock saddle, the other a McClellan army saddle. (SI)*

Whetstone and Spotted Tail agencies in Nebraska listed Smith and Wesson cartridge revolvers and Colt and Remington army revolvers in their inventories for 1873.[25]

The United States Army adopted the Colt single-action .45 caliber revolver with a seven-and-one-half-inch barrel in 1873. Over two hundred were captured by the Tetons at the Little Big Horn fight in 1876. These revolvers were stamped "U.S." on the left side of the frame.

Among the last pistols used by the Tetons were those issued to the Indian police. All specimens observed were Model 1875 Remington cartridge revolvers, and none of them were marked "USID." The butts of two Remingtons can be seen in figure 24, and two of them appear in figure 29. One obtained from the Brules was examined. It bears serial number 86. The left grip is hard rubber, taken from a Model 1890 Remington, and the right is made from a brass clock face, an interesting Indian repair.

Double-Barreled Shotguns

Though not a normal article of trade, double-barreled shotguns were supplied to the Tetons near the end of the time period under study. Government agents for various Teton bands during peace treaty negotiations in 1867 purchased six double-barreled shotguns bought for the Miniconjous, four for the Blackfeet, six for the Sans Arcs, ten for the Two Kettles, ten for the Brules, and four for the Oglalas.[26]

Arrowheads[27]

For obvious reasons, steel or iron arrowheads quickly replaced flint, bone and slate points. According to Ben Black Elk, son of the famous Oglala holy man Black Elk, the Tetons were totally unfamiliar with the art of flaking points in 1876, so complete had been their acculturation by that time. The metal arrowhead enjoyed wider usage and variety of manufacturing sources than any other trade object adapted from the white man's technology. Some were certainly made by European and American cutlery firms and a large number were turned out by trading post blacksmiths, but the greatest proportion appear to be of Indian manufacture.

Lewis and Clark noted that the Tetons were liberally supplied with iron arrowheads in 1804.[28] Nearly every nineteenth-century Teton arrow examined in the course of this study had a metal point. That the Tetons made many of these points themselves is proved by an 1870 annuity order for one thousand taper files for making arrowheads.[29] As early as 1805, Tabeau stated that iron for arrowheads would be a good item to sell the Tetons.[30]

Some points, on the other hand, bear names of commercial cutlery companies, and a Fort Union inventory listed "617 arrow points" in 1851.[31] An arrowpoint in the Missouri Historical Society collections similar to the one shown in figure 30 is stamped "PCJ," for Pierre Chouteau, Jr., and Company. The specimen labeled figure 31 was found near Crawford, Nebraska. The tip is broken off, but "H. MURPHY" over "HARVARD, MASS." is still visible on the point. Other makers of points which may have gone to the Tetons were J. Ward, Rodgers, and J. Russell & Co.

Dr. George Metcalf, now retired from the Smithsonian Institution, stated that he had observed a package of steel points from a trader's store in Montana. They were wrapped in white paper, a dozen to the package, and tied with white string. W. P. Clark, chief of scouts at Fort Robinson, Nebraska, in the 1870s, wrote that "nearly all the wild Indians now use steel arrowheads, they being a great article of trade among the savages. There are firms in the East who manufacture many hundreds of thousands every year and send them out to traders who sell them to the Indians for furs."[32]

figure 30. Diamond-shaped arrowhead similar to those sold by the Chouteau Company. (HDC)

figure 31. Commercial arrowhead made in Harvard, Massachusetts. (HDC)

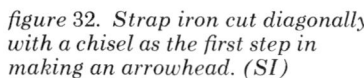

figure 32. Strap iron cut diagonally with a chisel as the first step in making an arrowhead. (SI)

If a point appears to be well made, it is probable that it was produced by a blacksmith or a cutler; most, but not all, Indian-made arrowheads are crude and asymmetrical. A good many of the iron axes from the Upper Missouri exhibit surfaces marred by concentrations of chisel cuts, which are most likely the result of industrious Plains Indians cutting out arrowheads. An example of a piece of strap iron which has been cut diagonally as the first step in making an arrowhead (fig. 32) is in the Smithsonian Institution.

George Catlin, who spent considerable time with the Plains Indians in the 1830s, made the following comments on arrowheads:

> Their arrows are headed with flints or bones, of their own construction, or with steel, as they are now chiefly furnished by the fur traders quite to the Rocky Mountains. The quiver . . . is a magazine of these deadly weapons, and generally of two varieties. The one to be drawn upon an enemy, generally poisoned, and with long flukes or barbs, which are designed to hang the blade in the wound after the shaft is withdrawn, in which they are but slightly glued; —the other to be used for their game, with the blade firmly fastened to the shaft, and the flukes inverted; that it may easily be drawn from the wound, and used on future occasions.[33]

This is reinforced by W. P. Clark, who forty years later observed that

> to make war arrows, the Indians manufacture the shafts the same as for game arrows. The head is then fastened loosely in the wood, and when it is fired into the body it cannot be got out. If you pull at the shaft the barbs catch and the shaft pulls off, leaving the arrowhead in the wound. Some war-arrows have but one barb, and when this arrow is fired into the body, if the shaft be pulled, the barb catches in the flesh and the steel turns crosswise in the wound, rendering it impossible to extract it. Fortunately, but few Indian tribes now use the poisoned arrow.[34]

Strangely enough, there are very few points which answer the description of the war arrow. In all of the Catlin arrows at the Smithsonian, there is only one point which seems to fit it (fig. 33). It has been carefully made and shows the use of a grindstone in sharpening it. There are four raised barbs set at right angles to each other, the shank is square in cross section and tapered, facilitating its detachment from the shaft, and the blade's cross section is that of asymmetrical planes cut into convex surfaces. Another type of point in the Smithsonian collections matches the description, but is identified only as Plains Indian. This head is shown in figure 34. There is no tang, and the barbs are asymmetrically arranged along the edges. It is of superior workmanship, and was probably made by a blacksmith.

The points collected by Catlin differ from those of the Indian Wars in several ways. They are generally less regular in shape and form; usually, but not always, they are smaller; there is seldom a serrated tang or shoulder; and most have an inverted or square shoulder.

A great many arrows were collected from the Tetons during the Indian Wars. The iron points average three to six inches in length and one-half to one inch in width. Certain styles of points seem to be typical of the period. Most common are the triangular-bladed, serrated tang point (fig. 35); the single-notch tang type, which was quite popular in Catlin's time (fig. 36); and the triangular-bladed plain tang style (fig. 37). Two types less frequently encountered, but still common, are shown in figures 38 and 39. One is the serrated diamond point which

figure 33. *Barbed war arrowhead collected by George Catlin. (SI)*

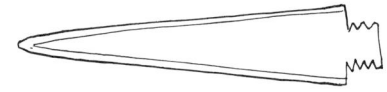

figure 35. *Serrated tang arrowhead. (SI)*

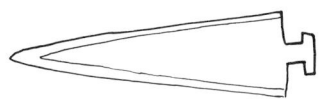

figure 36. *Single-notch tang arrowhead. (SI)*

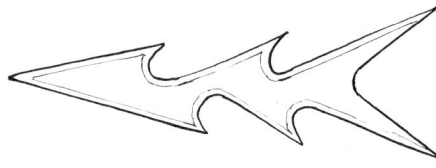

figure 34. *Asymmetrical war arrowhead. (SI)*

figure 37. *Plain or straight tang arrowhead. (SI)*

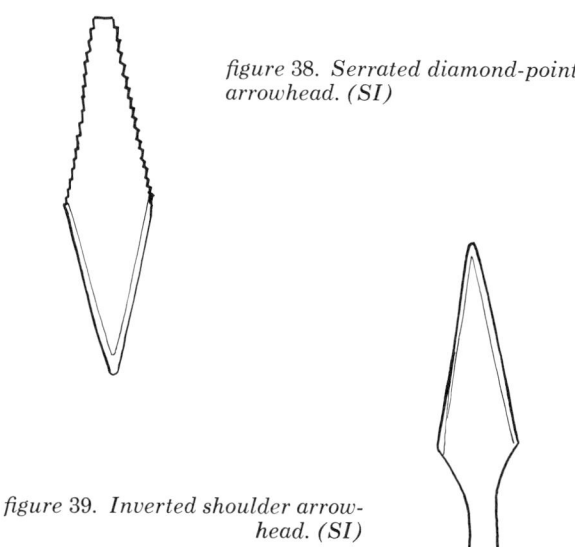

figure 38. *Serrated diamond-point arrowhead. (SI)*

figure 39. *Inverted shoulder arrowhead. (SI)*

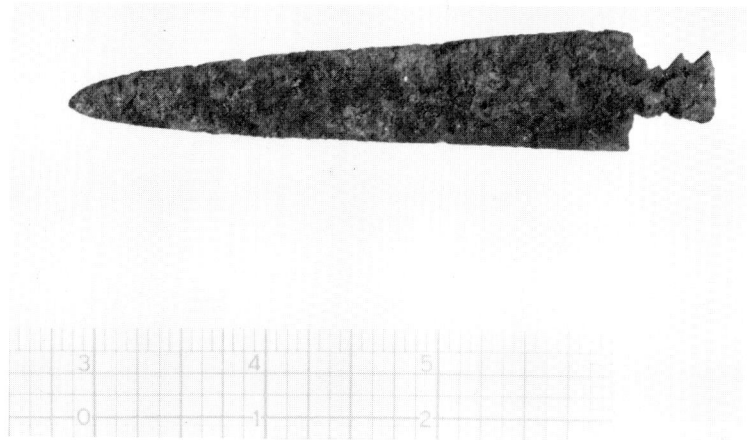

figure 40. *Arrowhead picked up on the Custer battlefield. (SI)*

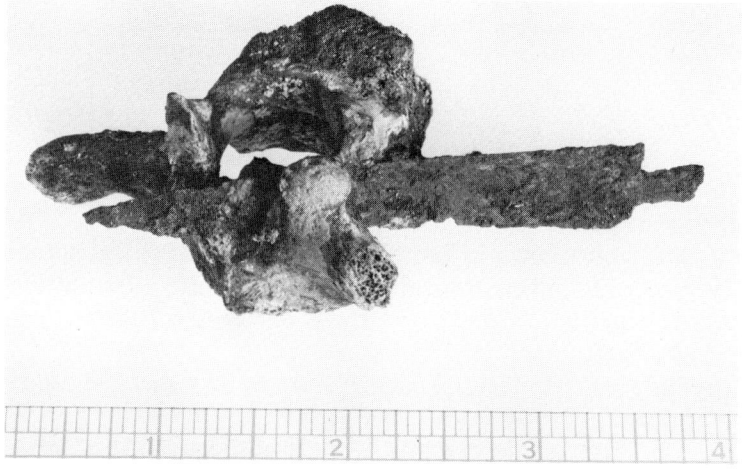

figure 41. *Arrowhead lodged in a human thoracic vertebra, found on the Custer battlefield. (SI)*

has long-toothed shoulders tapering to an extended tang. The other is the inverted shoulder point which possesses a short tang that can be notched or plain.

Catlin's and Clark's comments notwithstanding, it seems that while certain individual Indians may have used radically barbed, loosely attached heads in their war arrows, virtually all surviving specimens appear to be of the hunting type. Two points from the Custer Battlefield are shown in figures 40 and 41. One is still lodged in a human thoracic vertebra; it was picked up on the site about six years after the fight. Both arrowheads are of the type shown in figure 37, and both are in the Smithsonian Institution. It is quite possible that any arrowhead would serve as a war point because the sinew would

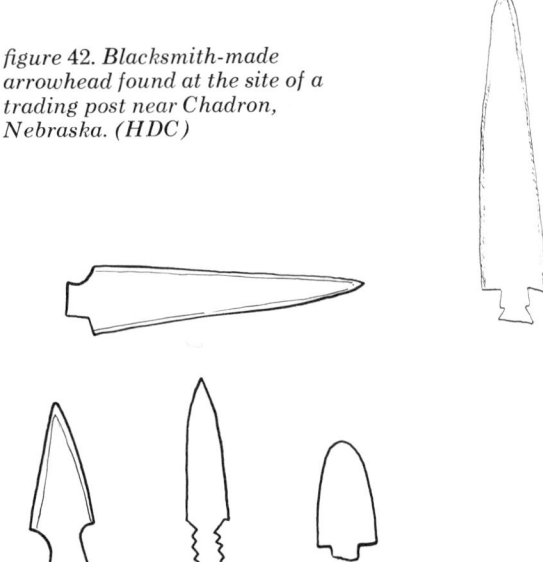

figure 42. Blacksmith-made arrowhead found at the site of a trading post near Chadron, Nebraska. (HDC)

figure 43. Arrowheads found in western Nebraska. (HDC)

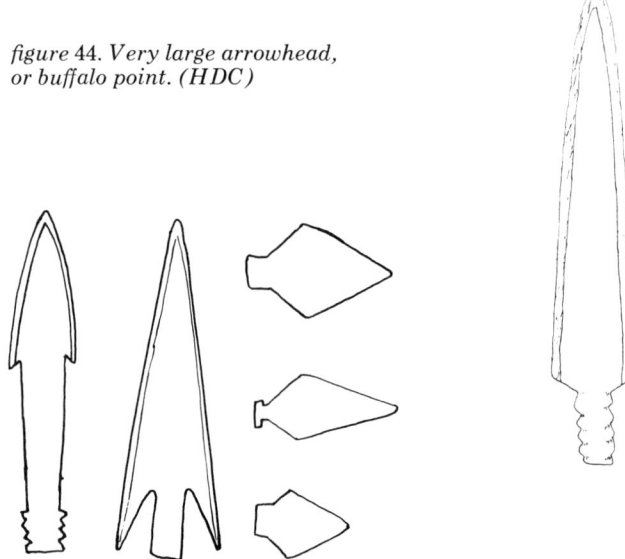

figure 44. Very large arrowhead, or buffalo point. (HDC)

figure 45. Arrowheads collected on the Upper Missouri by George Catlin. (SI)

relax and the glue soften when in contact with body fluids and allow the head to become detached.

The point shown in figure 42 is one of two identical points which were found in the ruins of a fur trading post, dating from the period 1830–50, ten miles south of Chadron, Nebraska. These are probably blacksmith-made because of the provenience, their lack of makers' marks, and their identical appearance.

The arrowpoints in figure 43 were all found in the Crawford-Chadron, Nebraska, area by Frank Dodd and Bill Hudson of Crawford, Nebraska. They provide some index to the wide variety of forms used by the Tetons. The example depicted in figure 44 is significant in that this is surely a buffalo-hunting point. Its weight would make it impractical for long-range shooting. My great-grandfather told of finding dozens of five- to six-inch points in the bones of buffalo along Nebraska's Republican River in the 1880s.

Figure 45 is a sampling of arrowheads brought from the Upper Missouri and now in the Smithsonian collections. Figure 46 shows a sampling of iron arrowheads found in eastern Wyoming; these are from the Museum of the Fur Trade collections.

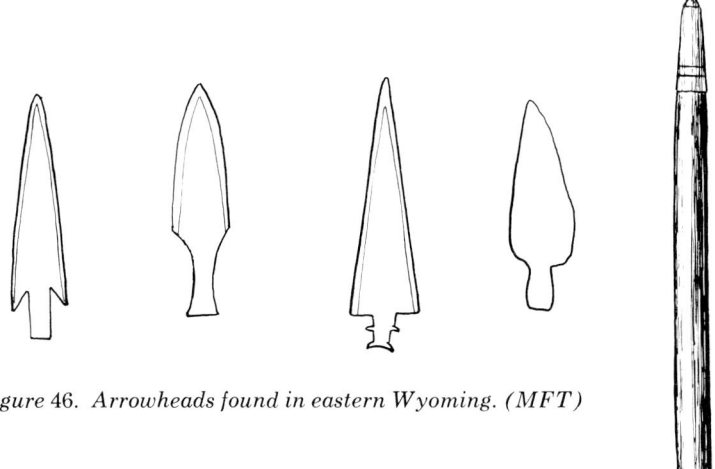

figure 46. *Arrowheads found in eastern Wyoming. (MFT)*

figure 47. *Commercial field arrowhead captured from the Tetons about 1877. (SI)*

There is a first and last in everything. About 1877, a Teton Dakota was killed in battle. His quiver and sinew-backed bow were taken as war trophies, and they were presented to the Smithsonian by Colonel William Boerum Wetmore, the famous Indian fighter. The quiver contained thirty-three arrows, of five different types. Six were made by an Indian, and the remaining are commercial target arrows of four varying but similar types. How an Indian got these is one of those mysteries that will go unsolved. The arrows are probably unique with regard to their history. All exhibit a shaft tapering toward each end, with fletching glued to the shaft. The nock is reinforced on each side with an inlaid piece of bone or ivory. The points are conical iron and about one inch long. One of the points is illustrated in figure 47. This is surely the last of the Indian arrowheads.

Lance Heads

Lance heads remain something of an enigma. While several known Teton examples were examined in this study, the early artists' renderings show curiously long or fluted points which are not commonly found. Normally, lance heads range from one to two feet in length and one to two inches in width. Figures 48 and 49 show two specimens drawn from the paintings of Catlin (1832) and Alfred Jacob Miller (1837). Those depicted in 49 and 56 may have been made from straight sword blades, possibly indicating an early Mexican traffic in iron spear points with the Plains Indians. A lance head found at Dayton, Wyoming, is made from a Spanish sword blade and is engraved "TOLEDO." Tabeau listed spears as trade items popular with the Tetons.[35]

After about 1830, the Tetons purchased lance heads manufactured either at trading posts or in factories. In 1834, the American Fur Company sent an order for "130 Assiniboin lances—as per sample furnished you by the Company the tang to be 2 inches longer and to have 3 holes in it for rivets at equal distances in the *square* part say 1 hole near the round part 1 hole one inch from the Extremity and the other hole half way between them—the price to be $1.00 say one dollar."[36]

An additional order was sent to Miles Standish, famed New York trap maker, in 1836:

100 Polished Russia Iron Indian Lances blade 18 inches long, 1½ inches wide at the heel and tapering gradually to the point, which is to be tolerably sharp—to have a ridge the whole length of the blade which is to be ¼ inch thick at the heel. The shank to be 5 inches long . . . with 2 holes . . . (also 200 Polished Rings to encircle the end of the Lance Pole, which is to be sound and 1¼ inch diameter—Rings to be ½ inch deep and ⅛ inch thick.[37]

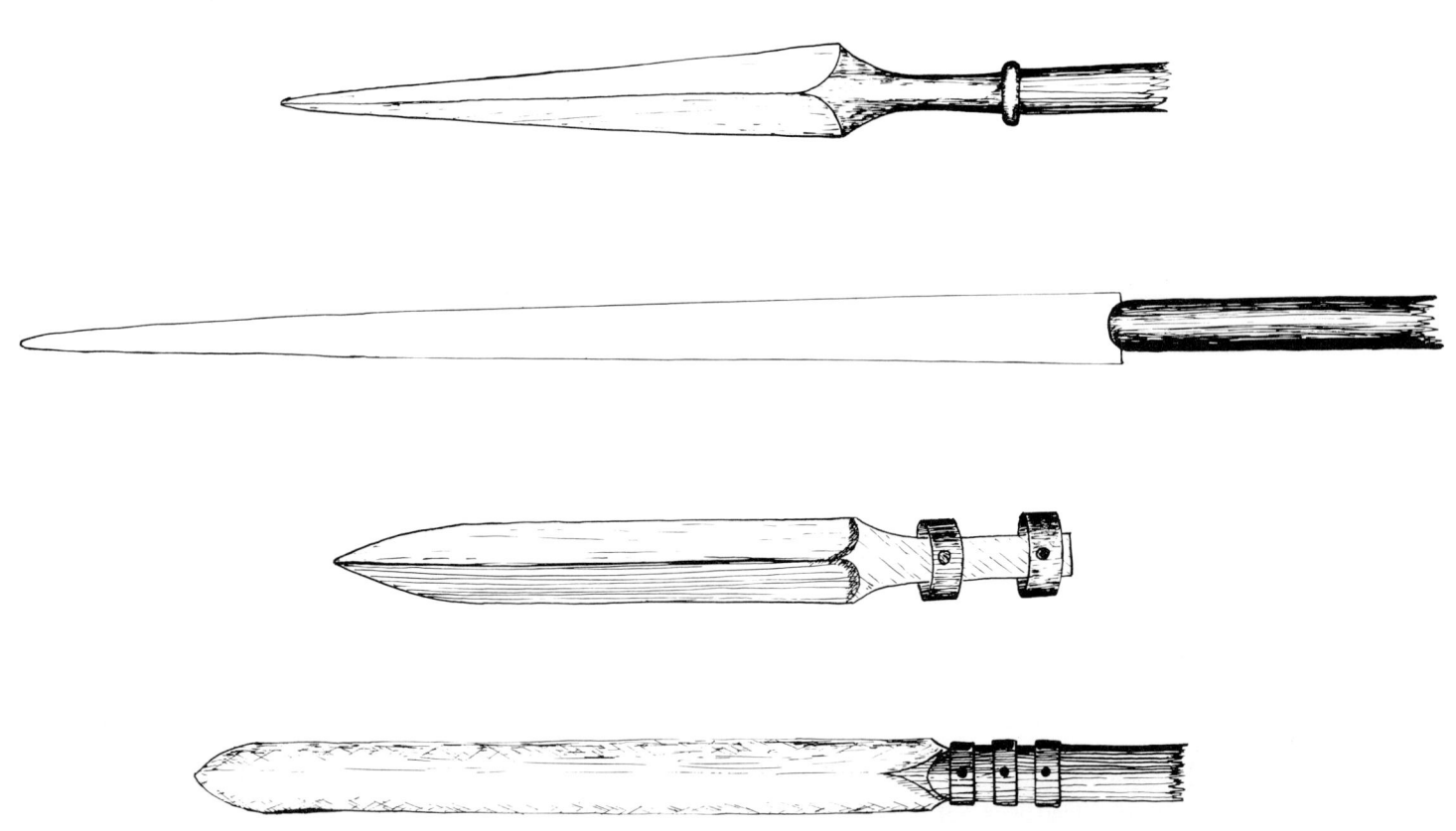

figure 48. Lance head, drawn from a Catlin painting of a Plains Indian warrior.

figure 49. Lance head, drawn from a Miller painting of a Plains Indian warrior.

figure 50. "Assiniboin" lance head with rings, found in Nebraska. (MFT)

figure 51. "Assiniboin" lance with shaft and three rings around tang. (MFT)

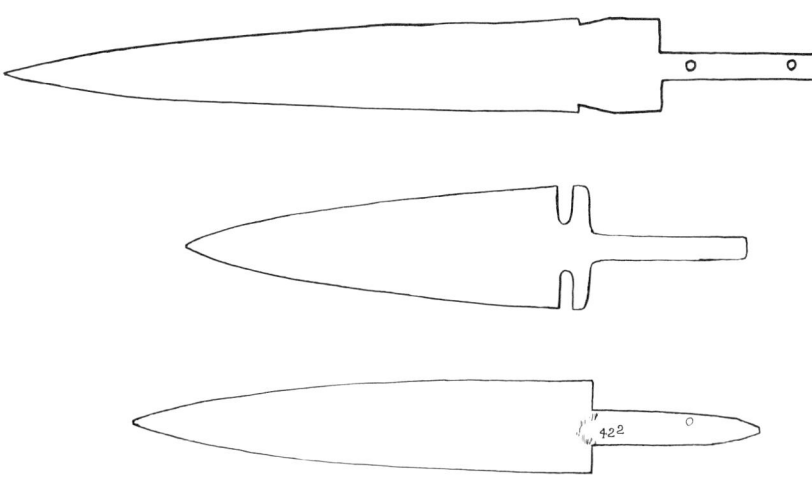

figure 52. Lance head, apparently made from a sword blade, found in western Nebraska. (MFT)

figure 53. Lance head from the Sioux. (SI)

figure 54. Lance head obtained at Fort Laramie before 1876. (SI)

This so-called Assiniboin lance must have been very common, for thousands were ordered by the trading companies. As can be seen from the above order, the lances came equipped with rings and shaft. A specimen which is identical to the one described in the second quotation was found near the Missouri River in a Nebraska cornfield. It is shown in figure 50, and still has both rings with it. Figure 51 depicts a shafted lance head which fits the first description. A lance head found in western Nebraska is illustrated in figure 52.

There are two lance heads in the Smithsonian which came from the Sioux. One, accessioned in 1927, is shown in figure 53. It is 12½ inches long and 2½ inches wide. The blade is convex in cross section, and is $3/32$ of an inch thick. The tang is $3/16$ of an inch thick. It appears to be commercially made, and bears some resemblance to the "dag" blades sold by the Northwest and Hudson's Bay companies.[38] Figure 54 is the second specimen. It was collected at Fort Laramie before 1875. The number 422 is stamped on the tang and there is also an off-center hole in it. The blade is convex in cross section, and is ¼ inch thick, 13½ inches long, and 1⅞ inches wide. The blade has never been used, and is still brightly polished.

Two interesting Sioux lances are described in the Army Medical Museum catalog. Unfortunately, they could not be located for study. One of them is thus described:

> A Sioux war-spear principally used upon the bodies of the wounded to discover if they were still alive. The iron head is six inches in length, by two inches broad at the base and is bound by iron wire to a handle of light wood four feet in length. The handle is ornamented with plumage of birds. . . . One of these spears belongs to each band and is held by the medicine-man, being inherited from father to son.[39]

This description seems to match the lance shown in a painting of a Teton medicine man (fig. 55) done by George Catlin.

The second specimen from the Medical Museum catalog is described as having a head "made from a straight bladed noncommissioned officer's sword. The handle is five feet long, and the head is attached to it with a buffalo hide wrapping."[40] Both of these specimens were collected before 1869.

As lances became less useful as war and hunting weapons, they seem to have become light and flimsy. At the Battle of White Stone Hill, September 3, 1863, between the Second Nebraska Cavalry and Saone and Yankton warriors, a lance was taken from the Indians (fig. 56). It was presented to the Smith-

figure 55. *Teton medicine man with ceremonial lance, from Catlin.*

34

figure 56. Lance captured from the Sioux during the Civil War. (SI)

figure 57. Lance with sheet iron head, acquired from the Sioux about 1888. (SI)

sonian Institution by Nebraska Territorial Governor R. W. Furnas. The handle has been sawed off. It is a polished hardwood stick ¾ inch in diameter. The steel head is bound to the shaft with sinew and then a buffalo tail has been sewed on and dried over the wrapping. The blade is ⅞ inch wide, 18½ inches long, and ⅛ inch thick. The tang seems to be serrated on each side for a distance of about 2½ inches. The edges of the lance are not very sharp.

Figure 57 is a specimen collected from the Sioux in the late nineteenth century. The head is thin sheet iron about one inch wide at the widest point, and is fairly sharp. The total length of the head could not be determined, but 8½ inches project past the end of the shaft. The shaft is ⅝ inch in diameter, and the head is bound to it with green and brown cord, wrapped over a piece of buffalo hide.

In the last years of the prereservation period any piece of iron which could be sharpened and would hold up under use was probably suitable for a lance head. I have also seen lance heads that were made from large, flat files sharpened on the edges, and believe them to be of New Mexican manufacture.

Knife Clubs

The most terrifying hand weapon used by the Plains Indian was the knife club. On a long, slender handle upwards of three feet long were two or three knife blades. (Knives used to make these clubs are discussed in Chapter 4.) The effectiveness of this in the hands of a mounted warrior riding at full tilt is awesome to imagine.

George Catlin does not show any knife clubs, nor does Karl Bodmer, who accompanied Prince Maximilian in 1833–34. The knife club may be a fairly late, possibly post–Civil War development. Its obvious antecedent is the gunstock club. Catlin painted many Indians holding these. The shape of the handle is reminiscent of a firearm, hence the name. These usually had a large blade, much like a lance head, set into the handle about two-thirds of the way up it. Catlin illustrates some of these with multiple blades. The Tetons may have used them when they were in close association with the Woodland tribes, but if so, they soon passed from favor on the plains. The Yanktons used both gunstock and knife clubs. Figure 58 is a classi-

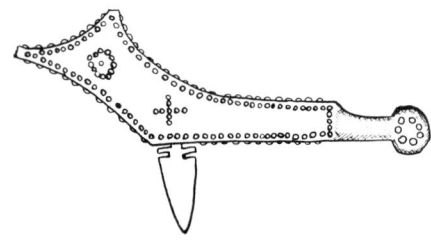

figure 58. *Traditional gunstock war club. (SI)*

cal example of the gunstock club, collected during the Civil War. It is not from the Tetons; virtually no specimens have come from them.

Figures 59 and 60 are transitional types from the Smithsonian Institution. The first was obtained from the Yanktons during the 1862 Minnesota Sioux uprising. The handle is thick and elaborately carved, unlike that of the typical knife club. It has three blades affixed to it. They are stamped "HENRY H. TAYLOR / & BROTHER / SHEFFIELD" and are high-quality butcher knife blades held in with iron pins. The handle is painted red and is decorated with eagle feathers, iron wire, and red cloth. The overall length is 38¼ inches. This specimen is reputed to have been used to kill a man during the Minnesota massacre. The second specimen was collected by Lieutenant Colonel D. H. Brotherton. It was taken from One Knife, who was probably a Hunkpapa. The handle is typical of knife clubs, but the blade is the style usually found on gunstock clubs. The blade tang comes through the back, and lead has been poured in to make a tight fit. The length of the handle is 44½ inches.

Knife clubs seem to have been most popular with the Te-

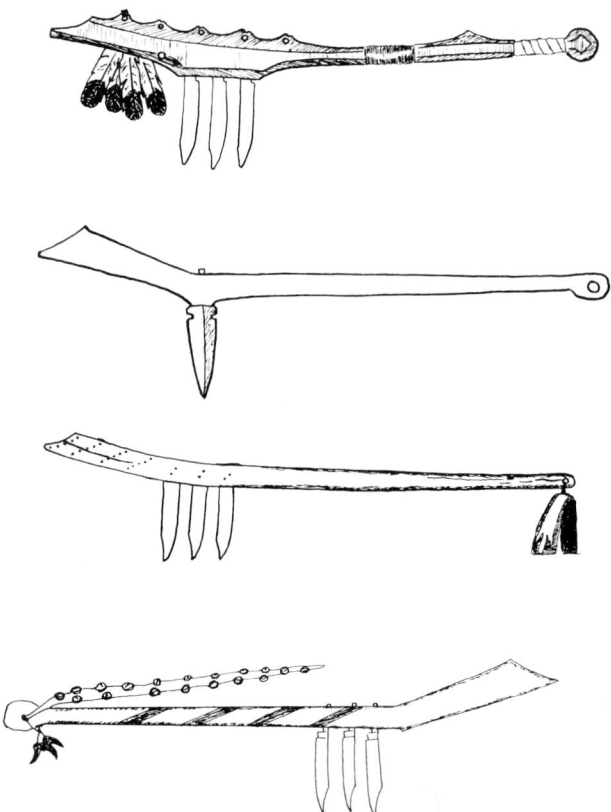

figure 59. *Transitional knife club from the Yanktons. (SI)*

figure 60. *Transitional knife club from the Tetons. (SI)*

figure 61. *Early knife club with Russell blades. (SI)*

figure 62. *Knife club used by a minor Oglala chief named Sitting Bull. (MAI)*

tons. Of those specimens examined, all were from the Dakotas, and most had been obtained from the Tetons. They seem to be as common as metal pipe tomahawks, and as a weapon, they were certainly more useful.

An early knife club is shown in figure 61. The blades are semiclipped-point butcher knives marked "J. RUSSELL & CO. / GREEN RIVER WORKS." The handle is painted red, and there have been four diagonal rows of tacks in the upper sides. The blades are held in the handle with two iron pins through each tang. A long, continuous groove has been cut in the belly of the handle, and the blades fitted in it. Then the groove has been filled with lead, iron nails and tin shims having first been driven in around the blades. An ermine, backed with red trade cloth and folded double, is tied to the handle through the hole at the bottom. The handle is thirty-seven inches long, $3/4$ inch thick, and one and one-quarter inches wide at the place where the blades are attached. There is a hole drilled through the upper tip, presumably for tying on decorations. This specimen, in the Smithsonian collections, was obtained from Stabbed Plenty, a Teton warrior.

Figure 62 is a knife club which belonged to Sitting Bull the minor, a secondary Oglala chief. The three blades are of the 1850 period and are stamped "MANHATTAN" over "CUTLERY COMP." over "SHEFFIELD." These are bowie knife type blades. The wood handle is flat-sided and has file brand decorations in diagonal lines. The enlarged butt is pierced for the attachment of three grizzly bear claws and a rawhide trailer, onto which are sewn a number of brass trade bells. This specimen, in the Museum of the American Indian, is forty inches long. Figure 63 is an L. A. Huffman photograph of a northern Teton, probably Miniconjou, taken in 1880 in Montana. The warrior posed with a knife club, similar to the one described above except that the wood is decorated with brass tacks. Another specimen

figure 63. *Photograph of Spotted Eagle, taken by L. A. Huffman in 1880. The upper half of his brass-tacked knife club is visible in the lower right. The three blades appear to be heavy bowie blades. (MHS)*

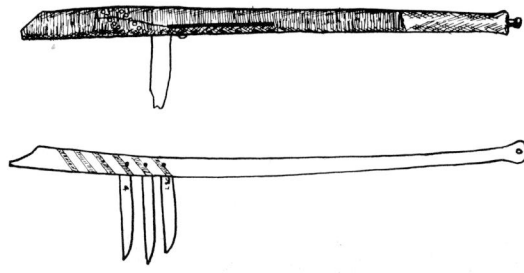

figure 64. *Straight-handled knife club collected in Montana.* (SI)

figure 65. *Knife club from the Wounded Knee battlefield.* (SI)

I have seen had three butcher knife blades stamped "FOX" with a fox and crown trademark. This piece was obtained on the Standing Rock Sioux Reservation in North Dakota. Fox may be a cutlery mark of the Hudson's Bay Company in the second half of the nineteenth century.

Figure 64 is another late specimen from the Smithsonian Institution. There have been two blades, but one is missing. The remaining blade is the butcher knife type, and is marked "LAMSON & GOODNOW MFG. CO. / PATENTED MARCH 5, 1860." The blades were set in individual slots, evidently with a drive fit. The handle appears to be oak, and is thirty-seven and one-half inches long. The lower portion is painted red for about seven inches, and the rest of the handle is black. A small knob has been carved at the bottom for attaching a wrist thong. There are two diagonal rows of brass tacks above the blades, and small notches have been cut in one edge below the blade. The handle is perfectly straight rather than slightly curved like those of most other examples.

A final example is shown in figure 65. It was picked up on the battlefield at Wounded Knee. The handle is painted yellow with six diagonal red stripes. It is thirty-eight inches long and has a hole in the lower end with a thong through it. The blades seem to have been painted red, and are fitted in individual grooves with one square pin through each tang. Each of the blades has been bent. They are not regular knife blades, but appear to have been cut from sheet iron. One is stamped "4" and another, "L & G." This example was presented to the Smithsonian Institution by Colonel John Rensellaer Hoff, the collector.[41]

Tomahawks

The tomahawk enjoyed some popularity among the Tetons. While they did not use them in great numbers, representative specimens from 1800 to 1880 have come from the Tetons, indicating that although their use was not widespread, it was at least consistent. Generally, the Tetons preferred long-handled, stone-headed war clubs for hand-to-hand combat.

Pipe tomahawks had a sharp blade on the front side and a bowl on the back for smoking. The handle of the weapon was also the pipe stem. Thus a pipe tomahawk was symbolic of both peace and war. While most of them are functional, as either a pipe or a weapon, they seem to have become, in later days, an ornament for a warrior to promenade with. Richard I. Dodge commented in 1882 that the

tomahawk is still in use, but reduced from its former high estate as executioner of the direful will of its owner, to a mere ornament, carried as a lady carries her fan. . . . Though there are yet many very elaborately ornamented tomahawks, they are regarded rather as an insignia of rank, to be carried on ceremonial occasions, but are scarcely thought of as weapons. Even as pipes, they are beginning to be voted a bore by the average Indian.[42]

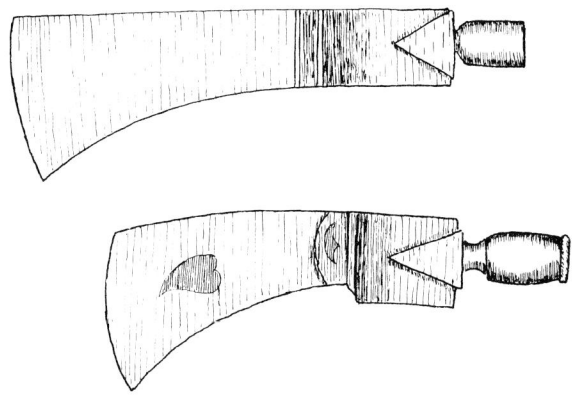

figure 66. Pipe tomahawk of the British pattern, about 1800. (MAI)

figure 67. Pipe tomahawk with silver inlays, period 1810, which was owned by Red Cloud. (MAI)

figure 68. Brule chief Wak-ta-geli, or Big Soldier, with a pipe tomahawk, from a Bodmer painting.

figure 69. *Low Dog, a Teton Warrior. The pipe tomahawk is the late plains variety with pierced, wide-flaring blade and tall, barrel-shaped bowl. His choker is decorated with brass tacks. (SI)*

William Clark, Indian agent in Saint Louis and formerly of the Corps of Discovery, in 1824 ordered six brass-bowled pipe tomahawks as presents for Sioux chiefs at Saint Peters, Minnesota, and on the Upper Missouri (these were probably Tetons).[43] He also ordered plain pipe tomahawks for other tribes.

The specimen shown in figure 66 is probably of British manufacture, period 1800. It is unmarked, with a round eye, and is nine and one-half inches long. It is a pipe tomahawk, and a similar specimen with a more slope-sided bowl is in the University of Wyoming Anthropology collections, Laramie, Wyoming. The pipe tomahawk labeled figure 67 dates from the period 1800–1825, and is reputed to have belonged to the Oglala chief Red Cloud. The eye is oval, and the bowl is slightly barrel-shaped. A crescent is inlaid at the base of the bowl. The haft, not shown, is maple with silver bands and diamonds. The head is eight and one-fourth inches long. Figure 68 is Bodmer's painting of Wak-ta-geli, a Brule chief, done in 1834. It shows a tomahawk which has a head approximately seven and one-half inches long and is typical of the period 1830–60. The pipe tomahawk depicted in figure 69, held by Low Dog, an Oglala, is typical of the Plains tomahawk of the period 1860–80. The blade is quite flared with a tall bowl. This style is ubiquitous among the Plains tribes. A fine example of this type of tomahawk, from the Smithsonian collections, is shown in figure 70. It was collected from the Tetons by an army officer before 1888.

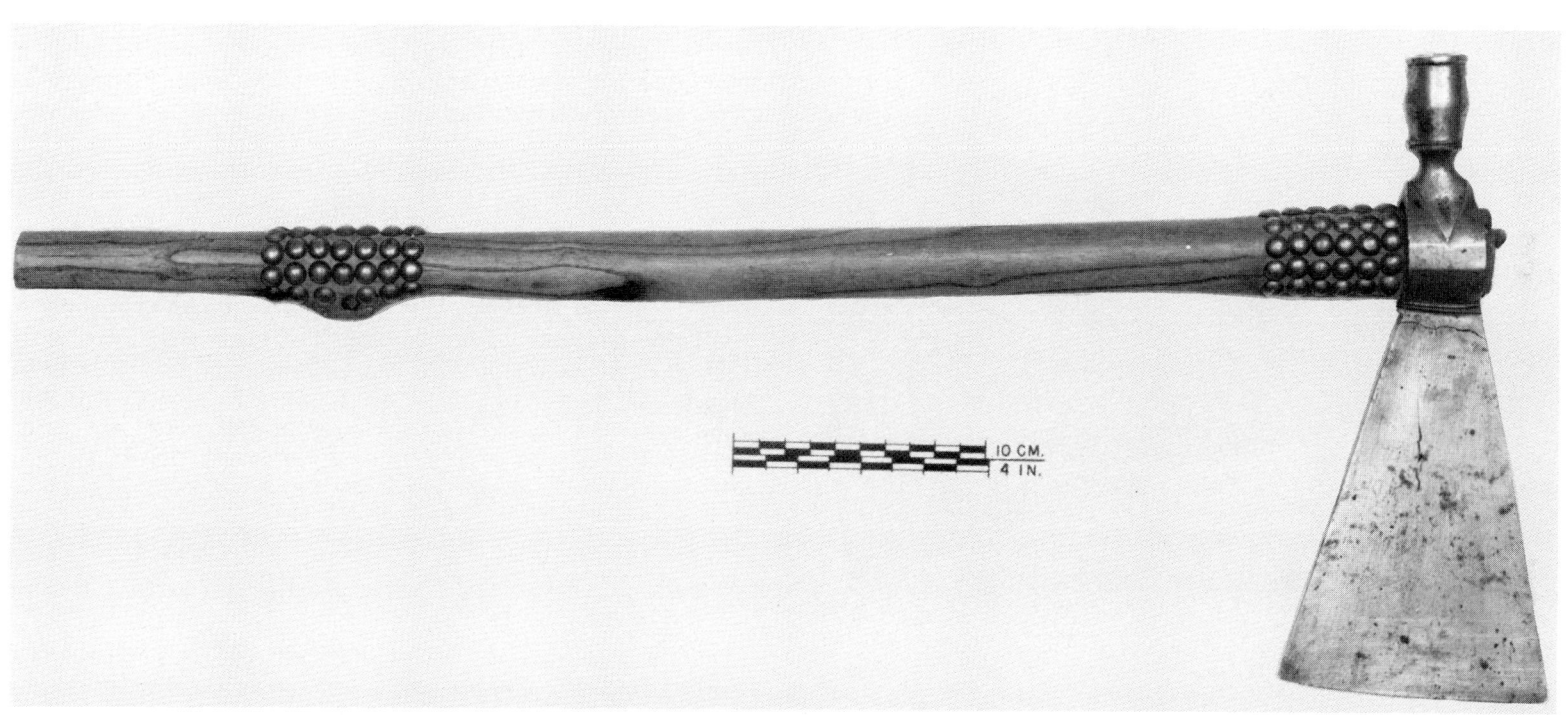

figure 70. *Late tomahawk from the Tetons, ca. 1880. (SI)*

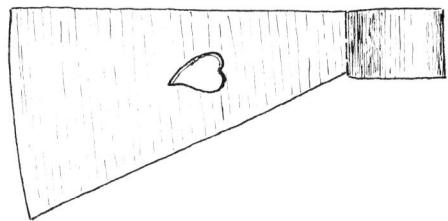

The so-called Missouri war ax, shown in figure 71, was, like the gunstock club, far more common among the semisedentary Missouri River tribes than it was among the Tetons. While the Tetons probably captured some in warfare, it is possible that they purchased them during their frequent trips to the Missouri in the early nineteenth century. A Teton winter count shows what appears to be an ax of similar pattern as part of the pictograph for 1814–15.[44] The ax head shown here has a round eye and is seven and one-half inches long. Figure 72 is a specimen which matches exactly Lewis and Clark's descriptions of the Missouri war ax.[45] It was found in western South Dakota. The blade has rusted through in the center. The eye is one inch tall with a blade six and one-half inches wide and nine inches long.

The spontoon pipe tomahawk shown in figure 73 dates from the period 1860–80. It is a fairly uncommon type, only a few Teton specimens being known. The blade is pointed with small curls on each side. It is cast of brass, and is eight inches long. Figure 74 shows a Sans Arc holding a tomahawk of this style.

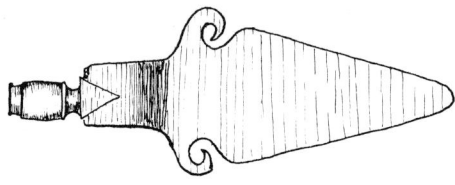

figure 71. *Missouri war ax collected from the Sioux. (MAI)*

figure 72. *A Missouri war ax found in western South Dakota. This is of extraordinary size and is quite early. The center of the blade has rusted through. (MFT)*

figure 73. *Spontoon-bladed pipe tomahawk of the period 1860–80. (MAI)*

figure 74. *A Sans Arc holding a spontoon, or "mini wakan," tomahawk. Note brass loop earrings. (SI)*

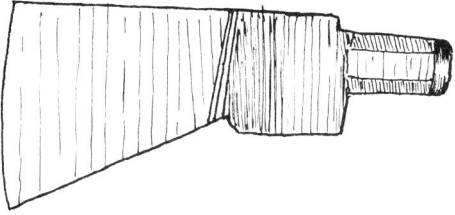

figure 75. *Tomahawk, period 1880, with a hammer poll in the place of the traditional pipe bowl. (MAI)*

Figure 75 is a representation of a very late specimen, circa 1870–90. Instead of a pipe bowl, the head has, at the back end, a hammer head, or, more properly, a hammer poll. These appear to be the last type of tomahawks used by the Tetons. They were more decorative than functional. This specimen, of cast iron, is six inches long.[46]

figure 76. Good Voiced Crow with a Civil War cavalry saber. (SI)

figure 77. Black Horn holding a heavy sword, either a European sword or an early American officer's saber. (SI)

Swords

Sergeant Ordway of the Lewis and Clark party mentioned that the Brules were armed with "a kind of cutlashes." He may have been referring to something like gunstock or knife clubs, but he may have seen swords used by the Tetons as weapons. Swords were sold to the Indians of the forested areas as far back as the seventeenth century, although after the introduction of firearms their popularity as weapons declined. They became symbols of rank for officers, and even the cavalry in the West dropped them after the Civil War as being ineffective.

Some Tetons did have swords, however. The mountain man W. A. Ferris saw several Tetons carrying sabers when he ascended the Platte in 1830.[47] Swords were occasionally presented to Indians at treaty councils, and a few must have been picked up by the Sioux in clashes with the army. Figures 76 and 77 are photographs of Teton Indians holding swords. The first, Good Voiced Crow, is holding what appears to be a regular U.S. cavalry saber of the Civil and Indian Wars period. The other, the Hunkpapa Black Horn, has a stirrup-hilted sword which appears to be a European military saber, but may be an early U.S. officer's sword.

Figure 78 is a drawing by Amos Bad Heart Bull of a Teton warrior society's regalia, which included swords.[48] A drawing from the Smithsonian collections shows a sword being carried by a mounted Sioux warrior (fig. 79).

figure 78. Drawing by Amos Bad Heart Bull showing swords used as regalia by a Teton warrior society. (From A Pictographic History of the Oglala Sioux)

45

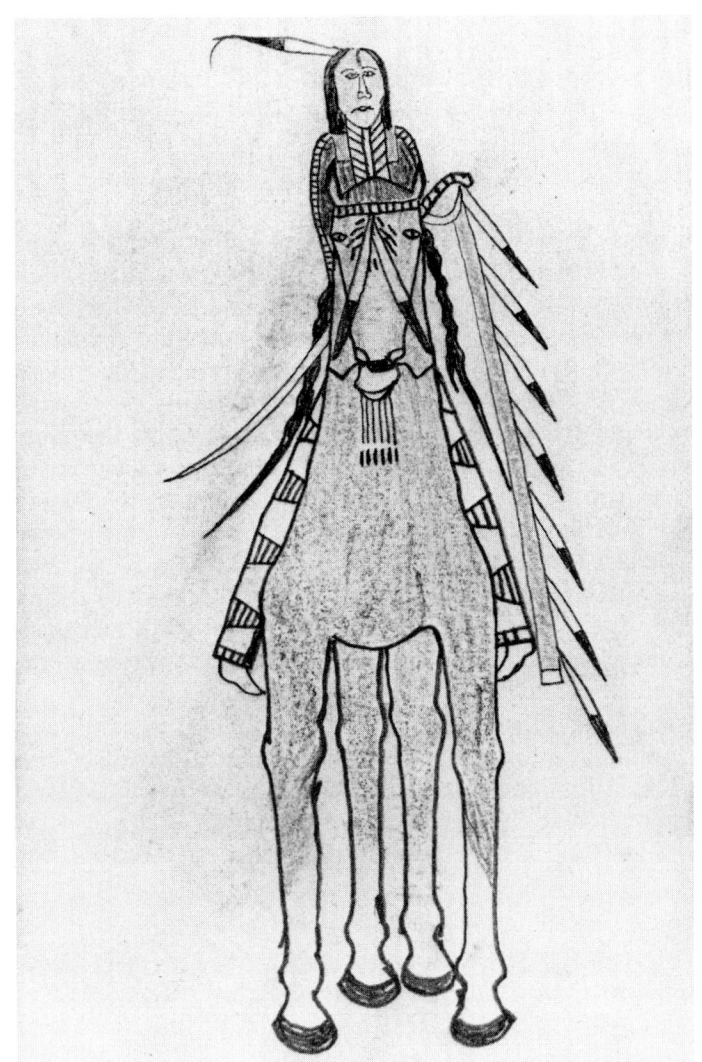

figure 79. *Drawing collected before 1890 showing a mounted warrior with a sword. (SI)*

46

Notes

1. E. De Girardin "A Trip to the Bad Lands in 1849," *South Dakota Historical Review* 27 (January 1936): 57.
2. *Annual Report of the Commissioner of Indian Affairs, 1852* (Washington: G.P.O., 1853), p. 65.
3. Garrick Mallery, "Pictographs of the North American Indians," *Fourth Annual Report of the Bureau of American Ethnology, 1882–83* (Washington: G.P.O., 1886), p. 134.
4. Ernest Staples Osgood, ed., *The Field Notes of Captain William Clark, 1803–1805* (New Haven: Yale University Press, 1964), p. 142.
5. Pike, *Sources of the Mississippi*, Appendix to Pt. 1, pp. 62–66.
6. Charles E. Hanson, Jr., *The Northwest Gun* (Lincoln: Nebraska State Historical Society, 1955), pp. 35–40.
7. Ibid., p. 49.
8. Ibid., pp. 26–27.
9. Ibid., p. 28.
10. Ibid., p. 25.
11. Ibid.
12. Contract Books, Office of Indian Affairs, vol. 5, April, 1844–March, 1845, pp. 67–69, 345; vol. 6, July, 1847–December, 1853, pp. 369–70, 475–76; vol. 7, June, 1853–October, 1858, pp. 72–73, Record Group 75, Records of the Bureau of Indian Affairs, NARS. (Record Group hereafter abbreviated RG.) For Henry orders, see Hanson, *The Northwest Gun*, p. 24.
13. Hanson, *The Northwest Gun*, p. 49.
14. Ibid.
15. Ibid.
16. John Parsons and John Dumont, *Firearms in the Custer Battle* (Harrisburg, Pa.: Telegraph Press, 1953).
17. Ibid.; see also *Illustrated Catalogue of United State Cartridge Company's Collection of Firearms* (Lowell, Mass.: United States Cartridge Co., n.d. [ca.1903]), pp. 84–85.
18. Col. W. A. Graham, ed., *Official Record of the Court of Inquiry concerning the Conduct of Major Marcus A. Reno at the Little Bighorn, June 25–26, 1876* (Pacific Palisades, Calif.: W. A. Graham, 1951), pp. 39–40.
19. Parsons and DuMont, *Firearms in the Custer Battle*, pp. 37–39.
20. John C. Ewers, *Indian Life on the Upper Missouri* (Norman: University of Oklahoma Press, 1968), pp. 175–81.
21. Parsons and DuMont, *Firearms in the Custer Battle*, pp. 35–37.
22. Ibid., p. 14.
23. Ibid., pp. 35–37.
24. Abel, *Tabeau's Narrative*, p. 117.
25. Charles E. Hanson, Jr., "The Post War Indian Gun Trade," *Museum of the Fur Trade Quarterly* 4, no. 3 (Fall 1968): 5.
26. Bill from Hunt and Co., New York, April 24, 1867, and E. G. Morse, Saint Louis, June 8, 1868, to United States Government for the Peace Commission, 1867, Letters Received, U.S. Department of Indian Affairs, 1867. RG 75, NARS.
27. Most of the material in this section appeared in *Museum of the Fur Trade Quarterly* 8, no. 4 (Winter 1972): 4–9. For information on bows and arrows of the Sioux, see O. T. Mason, "North American Bows, Arrows, and Quivers" *Smithsonian Annual Report, 1893* (Washington: G.P.O., 1894), pp. 631–81, and T. M. Hamilton, *Native American Bows* (York, Pa.: George Shumway, 1972).

28. Nicholas Biddle, ed., *History of the Expedition under the Commands of Captains Lewis and Clarke* (New York: Allerton Book Co., 1922), p. 132.
29. "List of Annuity Goods Required for the Grand River Agency for 1870," Letters Received, Upper Platte Agency 1870, RG 75, NARS.
30. Abel, *Tabeau's Narrative*, pp. 170–71.
31. "Inventory of Stock the Property of Pierre Chouteau Jr. & Co. U.M.O. on Hand at Fort Benton 4th May, 1851," *Contributions to the Historical Society of Montana* 10 (1940): 204.
32. W. P. Clark, *The Indian Sign Language* (Philadelphia: L. R. Hamersly and Co., 1885), pp. 48–49.
33. George Catlin, *North American Indians*, 2 vols. (Philadelphia: Leary, Stuart, and Co., 1913), 1: 37.
34. Clark, *The Indian Sign Language*, p. 49.
35. Abel, *Tabeau's Narrative*, pp. 170–71.
36. Order to Miles Standish, New York, June 10, 1835, American Fur Company's Papers, Orders Outward, vol. 3, p. 18, New-York Historical Society, New York, N.Y.
37. Orders to Miles Standish, New York, July 1, 1836, American Fur Company's Papers, Orders Outward, vol. 3, p. 137, New-York Historical Society, New York, N.Y.
38. Charles E. Hanson, Jr., "Hand Dags," *Museum of the Fur Trade Quarterly* 6, no. 1 (Spring 1970): 2–5.
39. "Army Medical Museum Catalogue," sec. 6, "Indian Curiosities, etc," MS, Armed Forces Institute of Pathology Museum, Washington, D.C.
40. Ibid.
41. For other objects from the same source, see George Metcalf, "Two Relics of the Wounded Knee Massacre," *Museum of the Fur Trade Quarterly* 2, no. 4 (Winter 1966): 1–4.
42. Richard Irving Dodge, *Our Wild Indians* (Hartford, Conn.: A. D. Worthington and Co., 1883), p. 420.
43. *American State Papers*, II, Indian Affairs, (Washington: G.P.O., 1834), p. 457.
44. Mallery, "Pictographs," p. 109.
45. Carl P. Russell, *Firearms, Traps, and Tools of the Mountain Men* (New York: Alfred A. Knopf, 1967), p. 286.
46. Data concerning all of the above specimens of tomahawks except those shown in figures 68, 69, 70, 72, and 73 were included in Harold L. Peterson, *American Indian Tomahawks* (New York: Museum of the American Indian / Heye Foundation, 1965).
47. W. A. Ferris, *Life in the Rocky Mountains* (Denver: Old West Publishing Co., 1940), p. 27.
48. Amos Bad Heart Bull and Helen H. Blish, *A Pictographic History of the Oglala Sioux* (Lincoln: University of Nebraska Press, 1967), p. 104.

Chapter Four
Metal Tools

Most of the metal tools acquired by the Tetons replaced stone or bone implements which were a part of their prehistoric culture. Firearms and horse equipment are notable exceptions to this generalization, but knives, kettles, scrapers, arrowheads —in short, the bulk of their metal implements in the nineteenth century—were acquired at varying rates to take the place of native-manufactured items. Undoubtedly, the Indian was most pleased with the trader for his unique ability to produce from his packs all sorts of marvelous tools which the Indian could use in his day-to-day existence. They brought a profusion of iron and brasswork to the Tetons. In a very few years the old flint-chipping and stoneworking arts of the Tetons had all but vanished.

Knives

The acquisition of the knife by the Tetons constituted an extremely important event. Until then, the Tetons possessed no suitable cutting instrument except the fragile and tediously made flint knife. Some anthropologists contend that a culture may be judged by the type of its cutting tools. If this criterion is used in judging the Tetons, they managed to leap over a thousand years of normal development when they first made contact with white traders.

figure 80. Eighteenth-century drawing of a Sioux with knife and sheath suspended around his neck, after Carver.

Tabeau remarked that, as well as regular knives, ones with green handles were popular with the Tetons.[1] "Green handled butcher knives" are listed in the Fort Union inventory for 1832.[2] These probably have handles of dyed bone, but I have seen no specimens from the Tetons. Possibly the coloring faded over the years of use.

Jonathan Carver did a portrait of a Sioux (fig. 80) in the 1760s which shows him wearing his knife suspended around the neck, as Miller saw the Tetons doing in the following century.[3] Knives were also carried in sheaths attached to the type of belt illustrated in figure 81.

The standard trade knife used by the Tetons was the common butcher knife of the period. While knives were probably traded at the time of earliest contact, the first positive identification of type and maker of the knives sold in the trade is probably that given by George Catlin in 1832. He wrote:

> The scalping knife . . . is a cheap and common butcher knife with one edge, manufactured at Sheffield, England, perhaps for sixpence; and sold to the poor Indian in these wild regions for a horse. . . . Every one in my collection and nearly every one that is to be seen in the Indian country to the Rocky Mountains . . . bears on its blade the impress of G.R. [for Georgius Rex, King George of England].[4]

figure 81. *Teton girl with brass-tacked belt generally worn with the type of sheath shown in figure 163. (SI)*

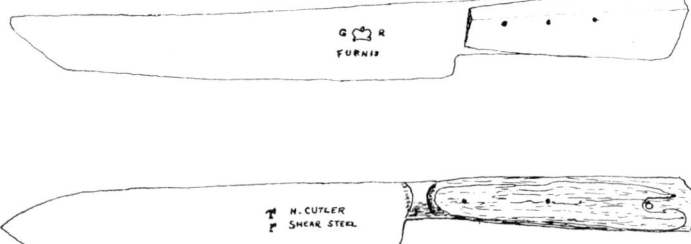

figure 82. *English knife by Furnis of the type described by George Catlin and ordered by the American Fur Company. (NPS)*

figure 83. *Knife by H. Cutler, found at a campsite on the Niobrara River in Nebraska. (MFT)*

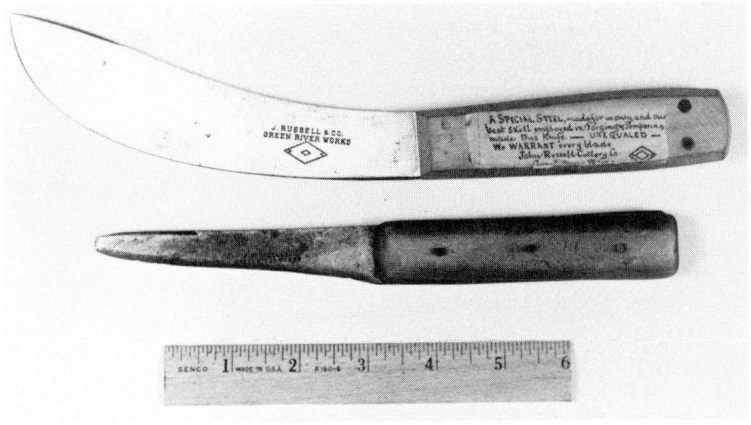

figure 84. *The lower knife is a genuine old Green River knife by J. Russell and Company, collected from the Oglalas. The upper knife is an unused specimen by Russell of the period 1880–1930. The diamond trademark is not found on genuine old Green River knives. (MFT)*

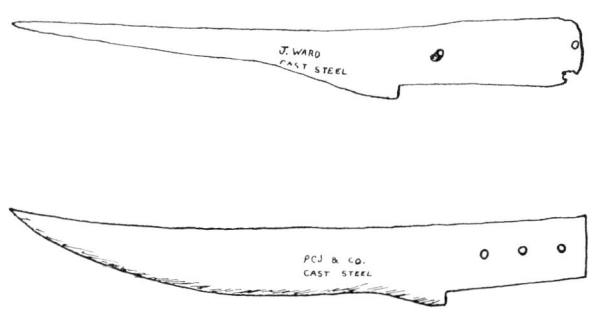

figure 85. *Knife by J. Ward, found in Wyoming. (MFT)*

figure 86. *Knife stamped "PCJ," for Pierre Chouteau, Jr., Company, found in Wyoming. (MFT)*

Figure 82 shows a knife which appears to fit this description. It was found in Jackson Hole, Wyoming, and bears the stamp "G-R" with a crown and "Furnis." Furnis made knives principally for the American market. Greaves of Sheffield is also believed to have been an early manufacturer of trade knives. The Furnis specimen is now in the Teton National Park Museum, and is probably typical of knives sold to the Tetons from 1800 to 1840.

The knives shown in figures 83, 84, 85, and 86 are all from the period 1840–50. Those in figures 85 and 86 were found in Wyoming, and the one in figure 84 was purchased from an Oglala by an army officer at Fort Robinson, Nebraska, about 1875. The example in figure 83 is stamped "H. CUTLER" over "SHEAR STEEL," and has a hammer and an "F" stamped in front of the name. Cutler was an English manufacturer who is known to have supplied knives to the American Fur Company in 1836.[5] This specimen has a spear type of blade, which is fairly uncommon for a trade knife, and has parts of the wood handle remaining. Figure 84 illustrates the famed Green River knife of frontier literature. The specimen has wood handles affixed with pin rivets and shows extensive usage. When new, the blade was at least an inch longer. The knife is marked "J. RUSSELL & CO." over "GREEN RIVER WORKS." The Green River knife was manufactured with this particular stamping until about 1870–90. The knife club shown in figure 61 has blades made by J. Russell and Company. Figure 87 shows a similarly

figure 87. *J. Russell knife with bolster. (SI)*

marked Russell knife from the Tetons. It differs from others in that it has a bolster at the upper end of the handle. The bolster is not solid, but rather is in two pieces and is set into the wood of each handle.

Figure 85 depicts a well-worn knife stamped "J. WARD" over "CAST STEEL." Ward was a maker for the Pierre Chouteau, Jr., Company in the period 1840–60.[6] The handle is completely gone, but one pin is still present. This is the only specimen examined which used two pins to affix the handle instead of the customary three to five pins used in other specimens shown. The example illustrated as figure 86 is of special importance. It is marked "PCJ & CO." over "CAST STEEL." I have seen Northwest guns and steel arrowheads stamped "PCJ," so marked to be sold by the Pierre Chouteau, Jr., Company of St. Louis, but it is certain that not all items sold by this firm were marked. This knife typifies the variety being purchased by the Tetons in 1850.

Two Wilson knives made in Sheffield are shown in figures 88 and 89. Orders for Wilson knives from the American Fur Company go back at least as far as 1827, when six hundred were purchased.[7] They were ubiquitous on the frontier from some time prior to that date until the end of the nineteenth century. The specimen in figure 88 is stamped "I. WILSON" over

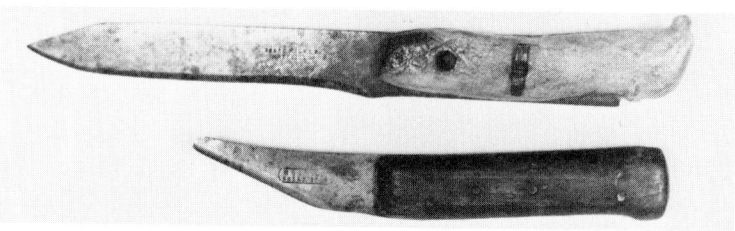

figure 88. *Spear-point knife by Wilson, Sheffield, England, with peppercorn and diamond trademark. (MFT)*

figure 89. *Two knives from the Tetons. Both are from the Brules. The upper one, with Indian-made deer horn handle, was made by Isaac Milner, Sheffield, England. The lower specimen is a very old and badly worn Wilson knife with early stampings in a cartouche. (MFT)*

"SYCAMORE ST." over "SHEFFIELD ENGLAND" and has a peppercorn and diamond trademark on it. It has the unusual spear-point blade. The specimen shown in figure 89 is typical of knives used by Tetons and frontiersmen in 1860 or 1870 and was obtained from the Sioux.

Figures 90, 91, and 92 were all found near the Wounded Knee battlefield in southwestern South Dakota. Presumably, these specimens are from the period 1865–90. The one in figure 90 is significant in that it is one of the few knives which has no maker's marks whatsoever. The name on the specimen

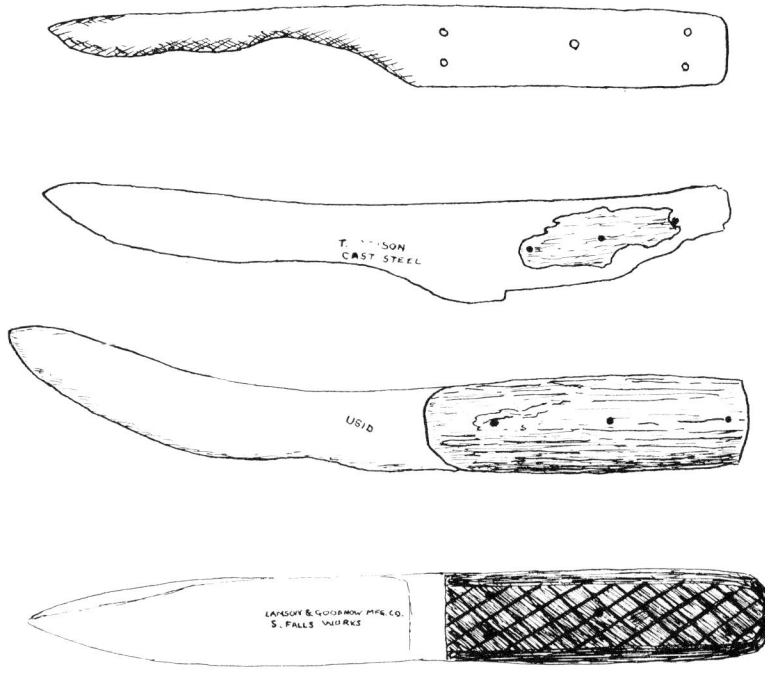

shown in figure 91 has been partially obliterated, but "T * * * SON" over "CAST STEEL" is visible. A portion of the wood handle is still attached. "USID" is stamped on the blade of the specimen shown in figure 92, indicating that it was the property of the United States Interior Department. While no record of any other knives so marked has been found, government cattle and horses issued to Indians were branded "ID" and rifles issued to Indian scouts were stamped "USID."

The 1870 annuity payments to the Oglalas included forty dozen regular butcher knives and forty dozen ebony-handled butcher knives. These were probably the products of the Lamson and Goodnow Manufacturing Company, which had many annuity contracts. The knife shown in figure 93 has a spear point with a checkered ebony wood handle. The blade is stamped "LAMSON & GOODNOW MFG. CO." over "S. FALLS WORKS." This is one of the last knives used by the Tetons in the pre-reservation period. One government order to Lamson and Goodnow in the 1870s was for 18,852 butcher, scalper, and hunting knives, and a large number were included in the cargo of the steamboat *Bertrand*, which sank in the Missouri River in 1865.[8] A Lamson and Goodnow blade is in the knife club shown in figure 64. A high-quality specimen in the Smithsonian, collected from the Tetons by Colonel D. H. Brotherton, is illustrated in figure 94. It is stamped "LAMSON & GOODNOW

figure 90. *Unmarked knife blade found at Wounded Knee. (MFT)*

figure 91. *Knife with partially obliterated maker's name, found at Wounded Knee. (MFT)*

figure 92. *Knife marked "USID" from Wounded Knee. (MFT)*

figure 93. *Knife by Lamson and Goodnow of the type given out as annuity goods. (MFT)*

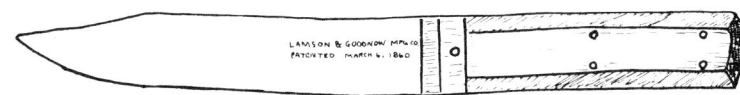

figure 94. *Lamson and Goodnow knife with bolster. (SI)*

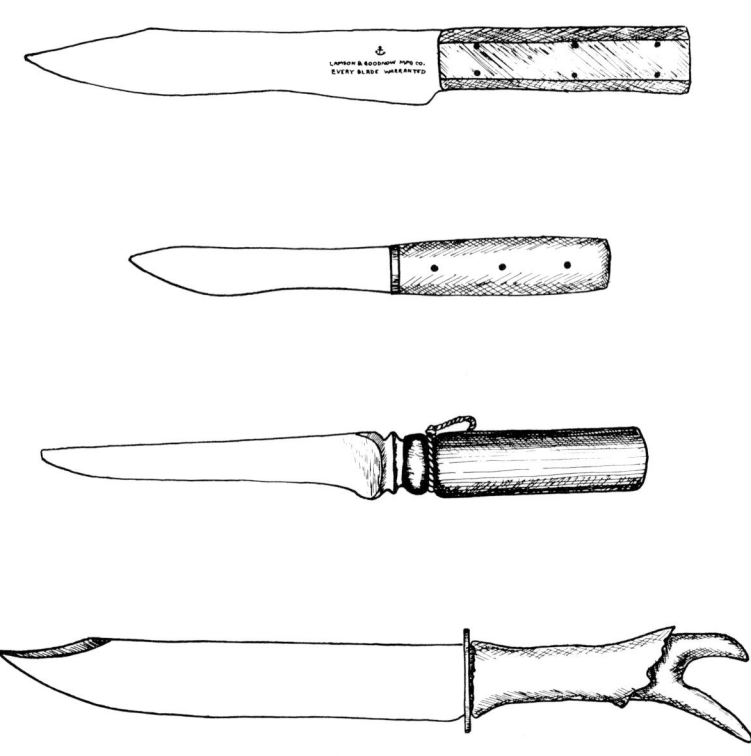

figure 95. *Very large and unusually marked Lamson and Goodnow knife. (SI)*

figure 96. *Butcher knife which supposedly belonged to Sitting Bull. (SI)*

figure 97. *Large carving knife with Indian-made handle, collected in Montana. (SI)*

figure 98. *Hand-forged bowie knife from the Sioux. (SI)*

MFG. CO. / PATENTED MARCH 6, 1860." The handles are affixed with five pins, and there is a solid metal bolster, probably nickel silver, at the upper end of the handle. The knife, somewhat worn, has an overall length of ten and three-eighths inches. Another specimen by the same maker from the same collection is shown in figure 95. It is fourteen inches long and was collected by the U.S. Ordnance Bureau before 1885. The blade is stamped with a fouled anchor, the maker's name, and "EVERY BLADE WARRANTED."

The example shown in figure 96 is reputed to have come from Sitting Bull. The maker's name is now illegible. There are three rivets in the handle, and the upper end of the handle is capped off with a flat nickel silver plate.

Figure 97 shows a specimen, obtained from the Tetons in Montana and now in the Smithsonian, which appears to be an old kitchen knife. It is badly worn and rusty, and the handle is handmade of cottonwood. There is a piece of cord tied around it, and the tang extends the full length of the handle, into which it is driven. The total length of this specimen is twelve and three-fourths inches. There is a heavy bolster forged into the blade.

A hand-forged bowie knife from the Sioux is shown in figure 98. It is sixteen and three-fourths inches long, with a brass quillon. The handle is deer antler, covered with rawhide. There is an iron rivet through the handle, and lead has been poured into the slot around the blade. This specimen is from the Smithsonian Institution. It was the only bowie style of knife from the Dakotas encountered during the course of this study.

Axes and Hatchets

Chopping tools aided the Teton woman immensely in the household tasks around camp. The axes received by the Tetons were of a standard pattern from 1800 to 1880. Some were made from flat iron (three-inch wagon tire iron was ordered for this purpose)[9] in blacksmith shops at the trading posts, while others were probably shipped to the posts from factories. The iron was heated red hot and hammered around a mandrel, a long, tapered iron pin. Then the blade was hammered flat, leaving a circular or oval eye. This style of ax is peculiar to the Indian trade, for the common ax manufactured for general trade was made from two pieces of iron with a flat back and a long, narrow eye.[10] Colonial Indian trade axes have an oval eye and straight sides.

Most of the axes from the Tetons are unmarked, but two marked axes were observed, one with "U" and one with "JB." The "JB" supposedly stands for "James Bordeaux," the name of a trader in Nebraska and Wyoming.[11] An ax marked "JB" is shown in figure 99. It was found at Cherry Creek, South Da-

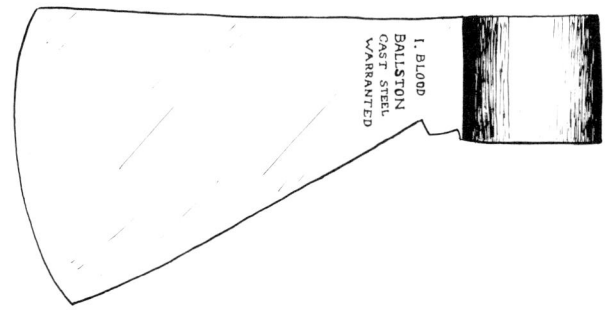

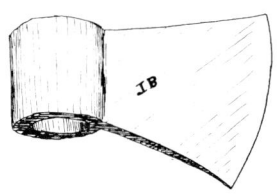

figure 99. Ax found in western South Dakota. "JB" is supposedly the mark of James Bordeaux, trader at Fort Laramie. (MFT)

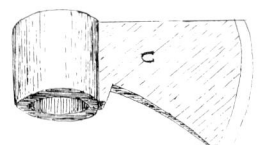

figure 100. Ax marked "U," from the Oglalas. (MFT)

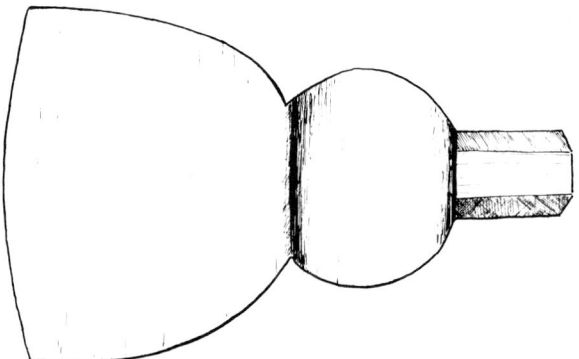

figure 101. Hatchet made by I. Blood, New York, found on Laramie Peak, Wyoming. (MFT)

figure 102. "George Washington" hatchet, drawn from a photograph, ca. 1865.

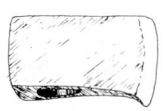
figure 103. *Hatchet head found on a Teton battlefield.* (MFT)

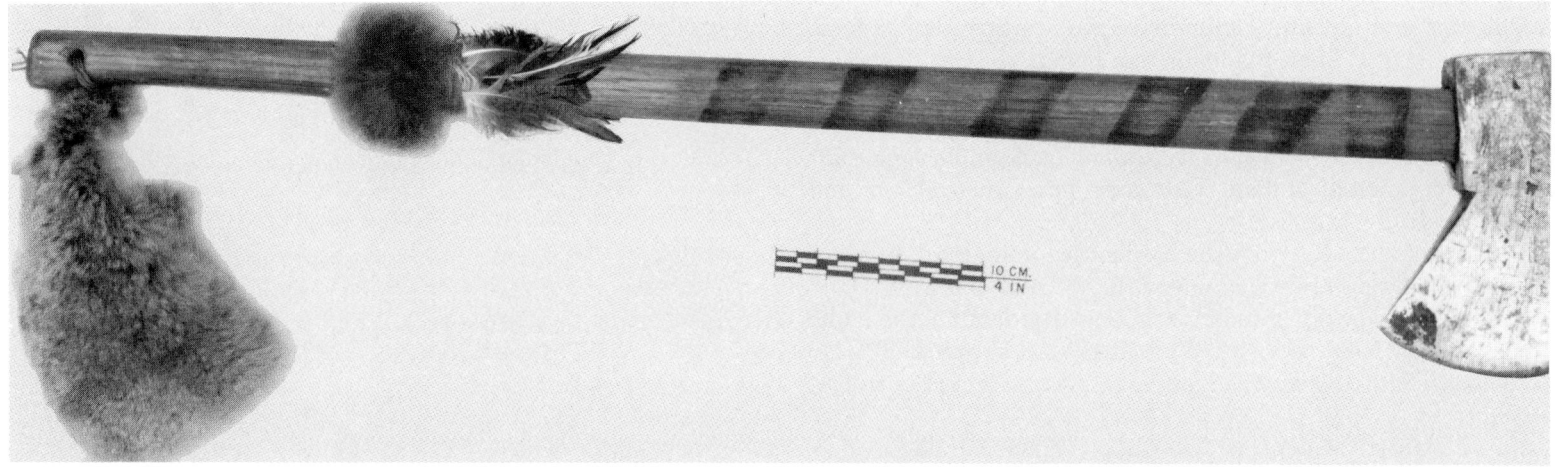

figure 104. *Half-ax made by Collins, Hartford, Connecticut.* (SI)

kota, and has been used as an anvil for making arrowheads. The specimen marked "U" is shown in figure 100. It was purchased from an Oglala woman at Pine Ridge about 1920. A similar specimen is depicted in Seth Eastman's painting of a Dakota camp in 1819.[12] In 1870, the Oglalas received six dozen axes as part of government annuity payments.[13]

Hatchets, like lance heads, are somewhat enigmatical. Whether or not they were used to a great extent by the Tetons is not known. One small hatchet made like the axes described above was plowed up in northeastern Wyoming. It is clearly marked "JMQ."

Figure 101 depicts a nicely made hatchet found near Laramie Peak, Wyoming. It is quite light, with an oval eye, and the marks on the blade are clear, reading "I. BLOOD / BALLSTON / CAST STEEL / WARRANTED." A number of photographs taken in the 1860s show Teton men holding the traditional "George Washington" hatchet. This style has a double flaring, symmetrical blade with a hammer poll at the back. One of these is sketched in figure 102. However, most hatchets with a history of Teton usage are of the standard "white man" pattern of the period 1850–90. The specimen shown in figure 103 is such a hatchet. It was found on a Teton-Chippewa battlefield. I have seen at least five similar heads among the Oglalas. A half-ax, or large hatchet, in the Smithsonian collections, is illustrated in figure 104. This was collected from the Sioux, probably Tetons, by Mrs. M. M. Hazen before 1892. The style of blade is called the Hudson's Bay pattern. It has a heavy, narrow, oval eye with a square back. The head is stamped "NO. 179 / COLLINS HARTFORD / CAST-STEEL WARRANTED." The handle is of Indian manufacture, with file-burned decorations. It is probably from the period 1870–90.

Cooking Utensils

Kettles

Kettles in the Teton culture date back at least to 1834 and probably to the earliest contact with whites. Yet however widespread their use may have been, Clark Wissler points out that the Tetons still remembered how to cook in paunches and rawhide bowls in the twentieth century, which indicates that the manufactured kettle did not completely replace the time-honored prehistoric utensils.[14]

Prince Maximilian mentioned the extensive use of cast iron kettles among the Brules in 1834.[15] Cast iron kettles were unusually popular among the Tetons. Possibly the Tetons did not object to their heavy weight because they had an abundance of horses to haul their belongings. Cast iron kettles were mentioned several times in the Pierre Chouteau, Jr., Company inventories and orders. Numerous varieties and huge quantities appeared after the Civil War as war surplus items and were dispensed to the Tetons by traders and government agents. The agent at the Cheyenne River Agency in 1870 commented, "The Army Pattern Camp Kettle is much better and more durable than the galvanized ones sent this year."[16] Among the annuity goods distributed to the Oglalas at Fort Laramie the same year were three hundred tinned kettles. Some of the chiefs objected to them, stating that "they preferred large iron kettles as used by the military."[17] Another agent pointed out that the tinned kettles imparted a metalic taste to the food.[18]

I examined a number of round-bottomed cast iron kettles which were collected from the Tetons. They were all similar in

figure 105. Army scout kettle found among items at Fort Robinson, Nebraska. The "IC" painted on the side is a military designation for "inspected and condemned." (MFT)

figure 107. *Thin sheet iron kettle with folded iron ears and loops for attachment of a ring in the back for pouring.* (MFT)

figure 106. *Late flat-bottomed cast iron kettle, or Dutch oven, probably annuity issue. The wire bail is missing.* (MFT)

appearance but varied in capacity from one to five gallons. Several collectors have commented that they are similar to army kettles, and this may have been their original use. An example of this type is shown in figure 105. It was among goods stored at Fort Robinson, Nebraska, before 1879. Another common type which I observed was the flat-bottomed covered kettle, or Dutch oven. Some of these are fairly deep, but most are shallow, being from three to four inches deep. These kettles have either three short legs or no legs at all. Some of the kettles are numbered on the lid (I have seen them marked 1, 2, 3, and 4), indicating progressive sizes. They have a handle on the lid and cast ears with a wire bail. Antique dealers generally date this style from about 1865. An example of this type is shown in figure 106.

Sheet iron kettles were common trade items. The example shown in figure 107 is typical of specimens collected from the Tetons. It has separately attached ears and a riveted ring near the upper lip of the kettle to facilitate pouring. The sheet iron kettle evidently came into vogue before 1836. J. A. Hamilton, a Chouteau Company employee, wrote to the home office in Saint Louis in December, 1835: "As our smith will be able to furnish the Missouri river with iron kettles please inform us of each size required for your posts and its dependencies."[19] The

the kettle was rolled; and all were stamped "AMERICAN BRASS KETTLE MANUFACTURING COMPANY" on the bottom (this firm operated in the 1860s). A one-gallon specimen of this type is shown in figure 108. These kettles are believed to be agency issue. The agent for the Upper Platte Agency ordered six hundred pounds of brass kettles from Poultney and Trimble, New York hardware dealers, in 1863.[20]

Skillets and Grills

Skillets were common trade and annuity items. Generally, the Tetons preferred long-handled skillets, but figure 109 shows a skillet which was reputed to have been given to an Oglala woman by the government in 1870. The skillet is unmarked and has a six-inch-long riveted stamped-iron handle. Figure 110 depicts the more common long-handled type.

figure 108. *The common brass kettle of the nineteenth century, widely used by all Indian tribes. (MFT)*

sheet iron kettle continued in use into the late nineteenth century; I have collected several late factory-made kettles of this type from the Oglalas.

Brass kettles were common on the frontier from colonial times until after the Civil War. Those sold or given to the Tetons were of a fairly standard pattern, but sizes vary from about one quart to about eight gallons. The kettles seen in the course of this study had the following features: the ears were cast brass and attached with two rivets; the bail was made of heavy wire; the sides flared out from the bottom; the rim of

figure 109. *Short-handled skillet with riveted handle. Possibly an annuity item. (MFT)*

Campfire cooking almost required a handle of this length because of the heat. The Chouteau Company lists orders for one hundred skillets with eighteen-inch handles and one hundred skillets with twenty-four-inch handles in 1836.[21] It is possible that fairly good lance heads could be made from the long handles. Old skillets were also cut up for arrowheads.[22]

Two rather interesting cooking stands or grills were found on the Pine Ridge Reservation. Both were considered to be relics by their owners, and they probably date from the period 1865–80. Both have four legs and are hand forged from strap iron. They stand about six inches high. One is shown in figure 111.

Coffee Pots and Cups

The Tetons, fond of coffee, used coffee pots and cups extensively in later days. Agent D. R. Risley at Whetstone Agency wired the Commissioner of Indian Affairs in 1873 and asked that 750 one-gallon tin coffee pots and 2,500 quart tin cups be sent in the spring of 1874. He said that the Tetons would prefer those items to the beaver traps he had ordered[23] (this tells something of the Tetons' attitude toward trapping furs for a living). Presumably, there is no difference between coffee pots and cups used by the Tetons and those made for other purposes in the same period.

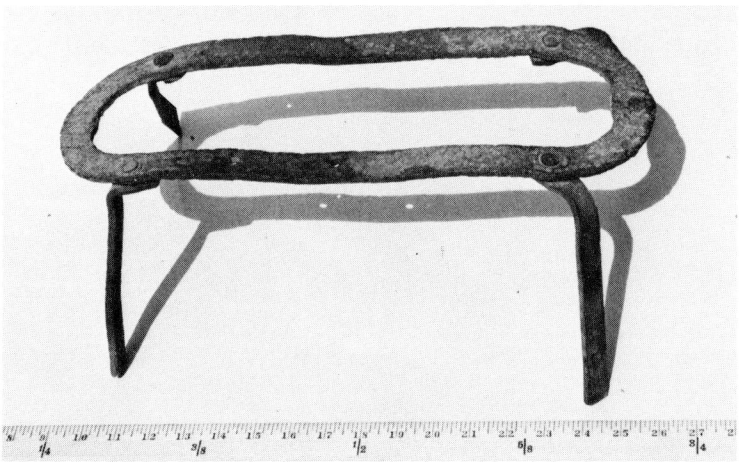

figure 110. *Old skillet with long, forged handle. The number 2 is stamped midway on the upper side of the handle.* (MFT)

figure 111. *Hand-forged iron grill or cooking stand, probably from about 1880.* (MFT)

Leatherworking and Sewing Tools

The Tetons, like all other Indians, were quick to adapt metal sewing tools to their own use. How early the Tetons began to purchase awls, needles, scissors, and tanning tools is difficult to determine. Probably they were in general use by 1830 and in abundance by 1850. In 1832 Prince Maximilian described how the Teton women fleshed an elk hide.

> The women were scraping off the particles of flesh and fat with a well-contrived instrument. It is made of bone, sharpened at one end, and furnished with little teeth like a saw, and, at the other end, a strap, which is fastened round the wrist. . . . Several Indians have iron teeth fixed to this bone.[24]

This shows that in 1832 both bone and iron scrapers were in use. By 1850, the number of traders, the Oregon Trail traffic, and the price of buffalo hides had increased to a point that the Tetons could acquire nearly anything they wished.

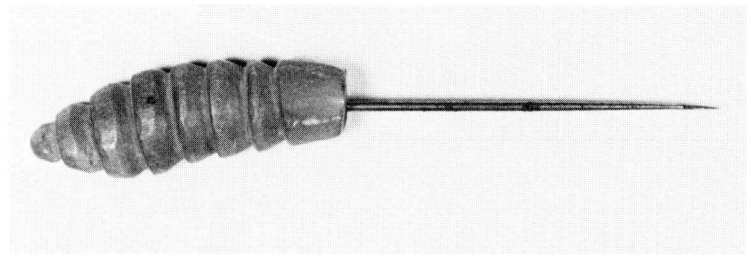

figure 112. *Round-bladed awl with mountain sheep horn handle. This is a very ancient specimen from the Oglalas. (MFT)*

Awls

Awls were a popular item that is still in service today among the Tetons. Lewis and Clark made frequent presents of awl blades to Indians. Usually, the blades were sold by traders and were fitted with a horn, bone, or wood handle by the Indians.

Figure 112 shows a very old Teton awl, dating from about 1850. The handle is carved from mountain sheep horn to represent rattlesnake rattles. The blade is round like an ice pick and is three inches long; the awl itself is five and one-quarter inches overall. Its historical value is greatly increased because of the handle. The mountain sheep was virtually exterminated on the plains by 1887.[25]

Two blades (figs. 113 and 114) illustrate the two most common forms.[26] The first awl is straight, three inches in length, and the blade is diamond-shaped in cross section. The second appears to be more functional. The blade is square in cross section, about four inches long, and has two ninety-degree bends

figure 113. *Straight awl blade with diamond-shaped cross section. (MFT)*

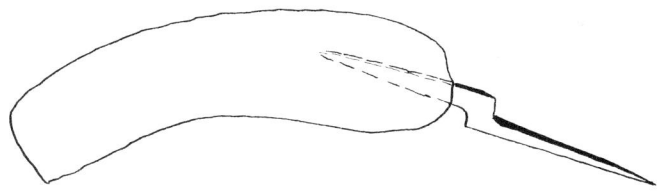

figure 114. *Crooked awl made expressly for the Indian trade. (MFT)*

in the middle of the shank. When in use, the blade would not gradually creep into the handle from pressure on the point. This is the typical "Indian awl" of the fur trade.

A very common adaptation made by the Tetons was to grind a worn-out butcher knife into an awl. I have seen at least a dozen still in use among the Oglalas. Figures 115 and 116 show two awls made from knives. The specimen in figure 115 was purchased from an Oglala, while the one in figure 116 was excavated at the Wounded Knee battlefield. It has been made from a Wilson butcher knife like those discussed in detail in the knife section.

Hide Scrapers

As mentioned above, Maximilian observed both bone- and iron-bitted hide scrapers and fleshers among the Tetons. The most common variety of hide scraper was made of elk horn. The main shaft of the elk antler was cut to a length of about fifteen inches. One tine was left at the end and was cut to about six inches and filed flat. Then a steel blade was wrapped and tied to the flattened tine. One specimen shown in figure 117 was obtained on the Standing Rock Reservation in 1938. The handle has been deeply worn from use and is yellowed from

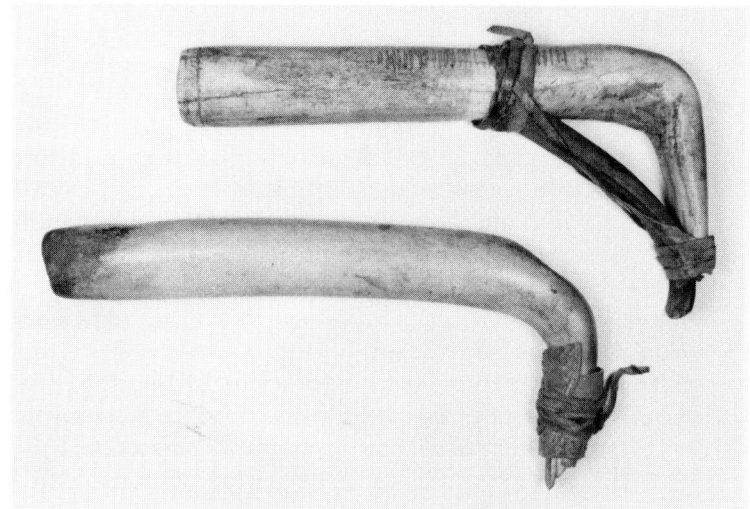

figure 115. *Awl made from a knife, from the Oglalas. (MFT)*

figure 116. *Awl made from a knife blade, from the Wounded Knee battlefield. The handle rivets are still in place. The Wilson name is clear, with the peppercorn and diamond trademarks below it. (MFT)*

figure 117. *Two elk horn hide scrapers. The lower specimen is typical of the Sioux, and came from Standing Rock Reservation. The upper specimen is from the Southern Cheyennes and shows a peculiar and highly functional bit which is tied to the handle in two places. This form does not seem to have been used by the Sioux. (MFT)*

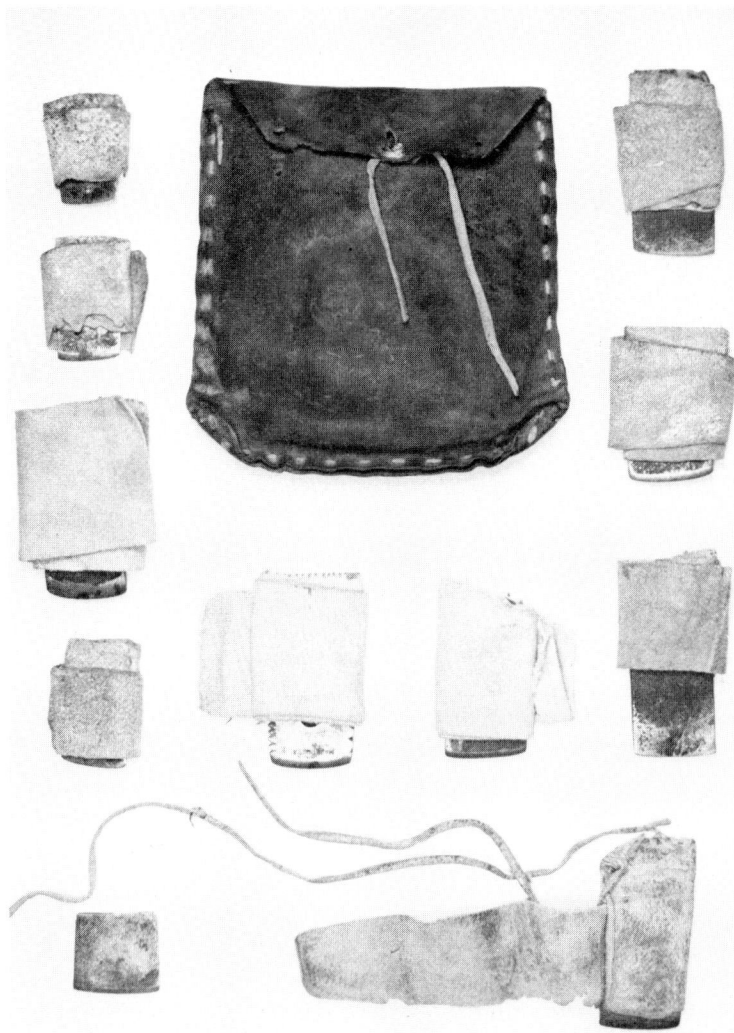

figure 118. *Bag and scraper bits from the Oglalas. (MFT)*

age. It must be an ancient one, for elk have been extinct on the plains since about 1880.[27] Thirty small circles have been carved in a row on the belly of the scraper. Mr. Forest Otis, the reservation storekeeper from whom the scraper was obtained, stated that these circles were symbols for each tipi made. Figuring one tipi per year, the scraper must have been used to prepare an amazing number of hides.

One piece, with ethnological significance, obtained from an Oglala is a bag of hide scraper bits or blades (fig. 118). The woman from whom they were acquired stated that they had belonged to her grandmother. The bag, made of commercially tanned leather, contains eight scraper bits, seven of which are sewn in leather covers with about one-half inch of the sharpened tip sticking out. One blade is sewn in canvas. It is made from a plane blade and is marked "DEFIANCE" over "MADE IN U.S.A." It probably dates from early reservation days. The seven buckskin-covered bits vary greatly in size. One is made from a mower tooth, one may have been made from a hinge, and the rest are made from strap iron. The smallest is one and one-half inches wide and two inches long, and the largest two inches wide and four inches long.

The Tetons commonly used old gun barrels for fleshing tools. The specimen shown in figure 119 is made from a Northwest gun. A Belgian proof mark appears on the top flat of the barrel. It has been cut off to a length of sixteen and one-half inches. I have seen several of these, all made in the same manner. The end of the barrel, where it was cut off, was hammered

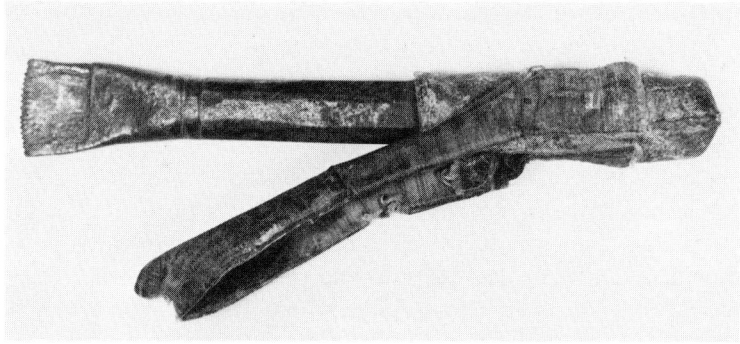

figure 119. *Fleshing tool made from a Belgian Northwest gun barrel. The hand is placed around the barrel just above the concentric rings, and the cloth loop encircles the wrist to help hold the tool perpendicular to the hide. (MFT)*

flat and teeth were filed into the flattened portion. Usually the other end of the barrel is wrapped with leather or canvas, to which a loop is attached. This is very similar to the bone scraper described by Maximilian. Of six specimens examined, five were made from Belgian guns and one was made from a barrel manufactured by E. K. Tryon of Philadelphia. Fleshing tools of this type are evidently being faked from old musket barrels by unscrupulous dealers.

A fleshing tool from the Smithsonian collections is depicted in figure 120. It was collected from the Tetons at Fort

figure 120. *Fleshing tool made from square iron rod. (SI)*

figure 121. *A collection of Sioux tanning tools. From the top, they are: scythe blade for scraping hair and superfluous tissue; peculiar hide scraper of strap iron with wood handles bolted on, made by the government blacksmith at Fort Yates, North Dakota, 1873; Miniconjou scraping tool, the function of which is similar to that of the scythe blade, with carved wood handle; a hand-held scraper made from thin galvanized iron. (KOL)*

Keogh, Montana, before 1893. The scraper is solid square iron with a hide covering sewn on. It is crudely forged, and the upper end is somewhat like certain types of railroad spikes. The total length of the tool is twelve and three-eighths inches.

Scythe blades were used by the Tetons to scrape the hair and excess tissue from hides.[28] It could not be determined when the Tetons began using scythe blades, but I have seen several still being used by them. I believe that because the scythe was an agricultural implement associated with farmers rather than with Indians, it was probably obtained in quantity during the heavy western expansion after the Civil War. A collection of tanning tools from the Tetons is shown in figure 121.

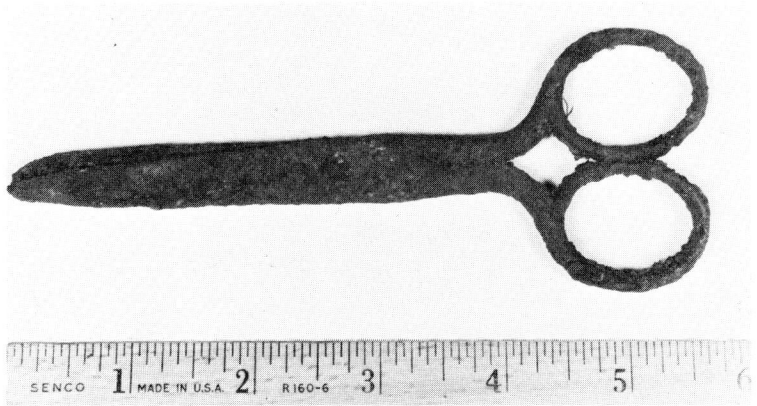

figure 122. *Scissors from the Wounded Knee battlefield, probably Miniconjou. (MFT)*

Scissors

Nearly every nineteenth-century Teton woman owned a pair of scissors. The advantages and usefulness of scissors over stone tools are obvious. The scissors of the period are generally rather small and are identical to those available in stores today. A typical pair is shown in figure 122. Large shears were given out as annuity goods; a pair of these is illustrated in figure 123.

Needles

Needles were a common trade item and were used for beading and cloth sewing. Since the manufacturing techniques and appearances of needles have not changed for 140 years,[29]

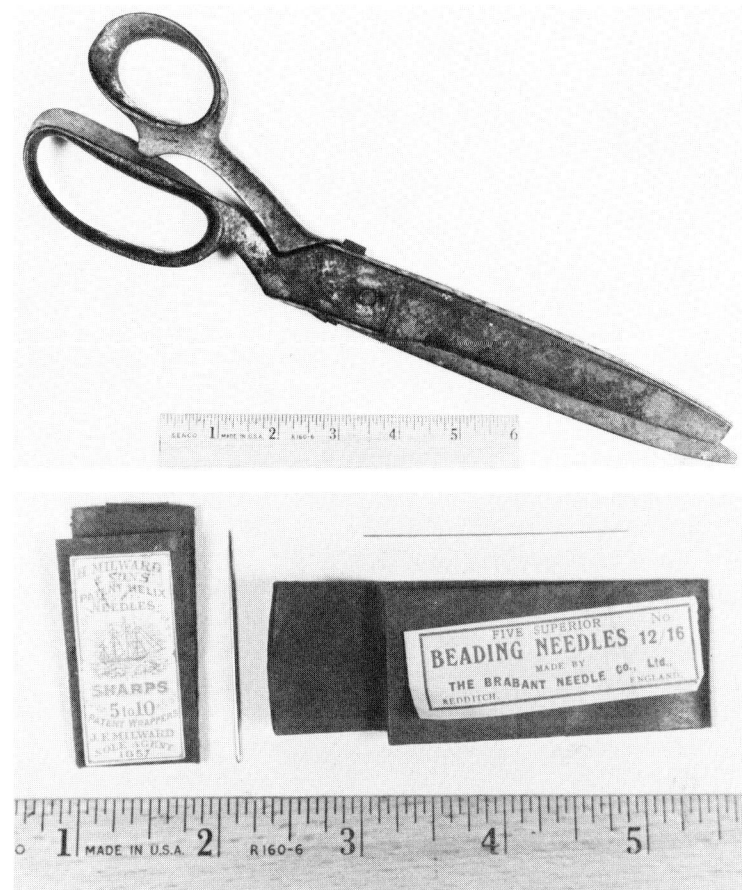

figure 123. *Large shears given out by the federal government as annuity goods. (MFT)*

figure 124. *Two nineteenth-century packets or papers of needles. A sample from each is beside the packet. (MFT)*

I assume that the needles available today are similar to those used by the Tetons, with the exception that long, fine needles were used for beadwork. The American Fur Company ordered regular, darning, and glovers' needles in 1827.[30] Two nineteenth-century packets of needles are shown in figure 124.

Quill Flatteners

One specialized tool developed solely for Indian usage was the smoothing iron, or quill flattener. It was used to press porcupine quills flat after they had been sewn on clothing as decoration. A quill flattener (fig. 125) was found near Sutherland, Nebraska, in close association with coins dated 1876. It is twelve and one-half inches long and is bent in an elongated S shape. The tips are flat and the center has finely forged decorative rings around the circumference. Another specimen (fig. 126) was collected from the Brules. It is shorter and has wider tips than the flattener described above. The specimen in figure 127 was collected on the Standing Rock Reservation and

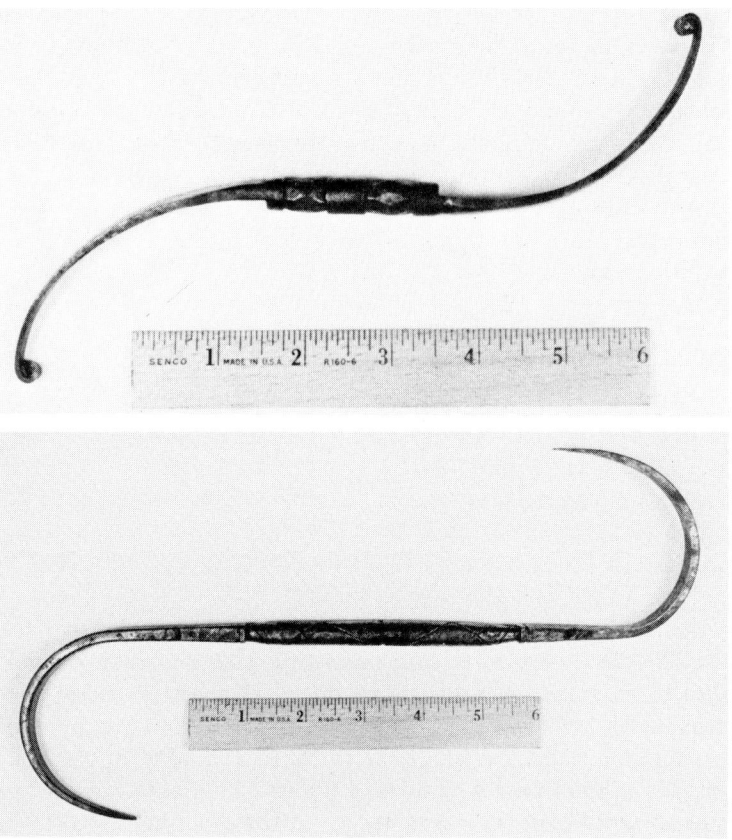

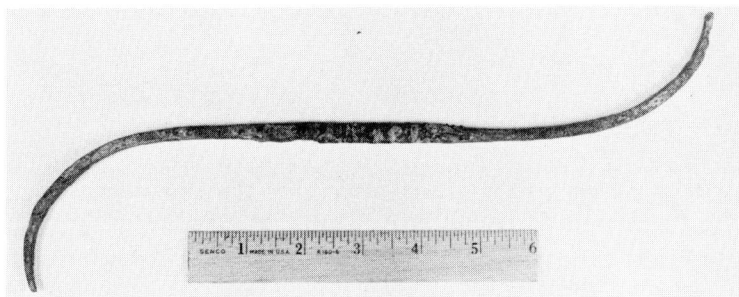

figure 125. *Large quill flattener, probably Oglala and definitely Teton, from about 1870. While it is badly rusted, the handle in the center still shows signs of intricate rings filed in it for decoration.* (MFT)

figure 126. *Very fine example of a quill flattener from the Brules. The flattened ends are three-fourths inch wide. The handle has been beautifully faceted by filing.* (MFT)

figure 127. *A very large quill flattener from the Hunkpapas. This may be a late specimen, with radically curved ends and rather simple filed decorations on the center part, or handle.* (KOL) has deeply curved tips of a somewhat aberrant form. Robert W. Neuman comments that quill flatteners were "being produced at least by the end of the first half of the nineteenth century."[31] This is probably true, and I surmise that heirloom quill flatteners were still in use in the twentieth century. Most known specimens have been collected from the Tetons. The tool was grasped in the center and the flattened tip at either end was used to flatten the round quills in a manner similar to ironing clothing.

Hoes and Spades

Hoes and spades are listed in the 1850 Fort Union inventories, but in such small quantities that they were probably not for general sale. The Indian agents tried hard to convert the Tetons into agriculturists after the Civil War, and the agent at the second Whetstone Agency for the Brules in Nebraska ordered garden seed and two hundred hoes for the Tetons in 1871.[32] I have acquired three identical hoes from the Oglalas. They have a socket at the top like the eye of a trade ax. The blades are a half circle of iron and show forging marks. On the backs are stamped two stars, one on each side, with the inscription "CLEMENT & MAYNARD" under one star and "WARRANTED" over "NO. 2" under the other. These "planter's hoes" are of a nineteenth-century pattern. Because of their identical nature and their wide distribution among the Tetons, I believe that these are the hoes issued by the government to the Tetons after the Civil War. An example is shown in figure 128. An unmarked specimen of the same general description was collected on Standing Rock Reservation.

It would be difficult to imagine the Tetons gardening without some sort of tool with which to till the soil. No orders for plows were found, and therefore spades were possibly used,

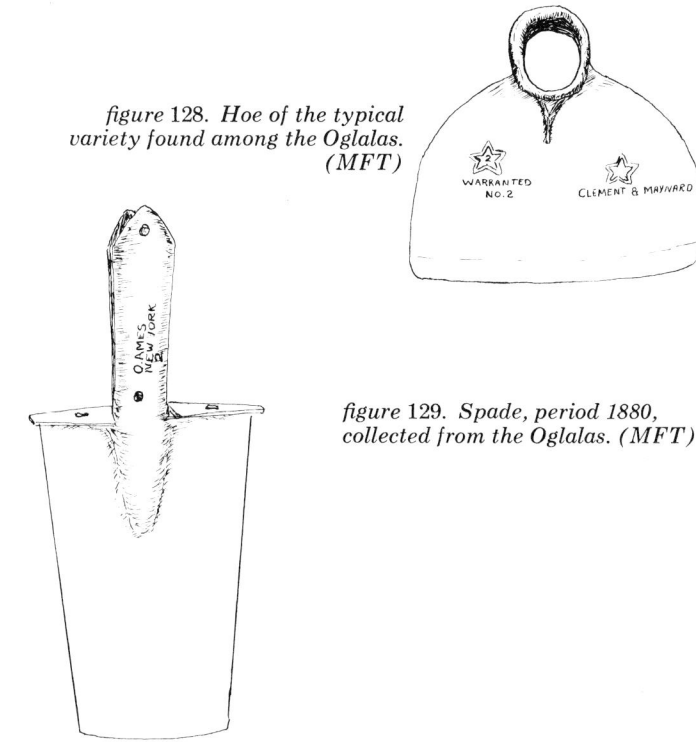

figure 128. *Hoe of the typical variety found among the Oglalas. (MFT)*

figure 129. *Spade, period 1880, collected from the Oglalas. (MFT)*

although no orders for them were found either. One early specimen of a shovel was collected from an Oglala in 1964 (fig. 129). At the point where the handle joins the blade the metal is stamped "O. AMES" over "NEW YORK" over "2." The blade is made of two rectangular pieces of steel forged together at the edges with extensions at the upper edges to form a handle socket. Foot rests one-half inch wide and three inches long are riveted on each side of the blade along the top edge.

Firesteels

Trading companies supplied the Tetons with thousands of "strike-a-lights," or firesteels. Carl P. Russell states that the Chouteau Company generally sold oval firesteels. Hiram Cutler of Sheffield supplied "Warranted Bright Oval" steels for thirty cents a dozen.[33] The oval firesteel is found from the earliest colonial to nineteenth-century sites.[34] The specimen shown in figure 130 was found in central Nebraska. It is oval, four inches long and two inches wide. The slot cut in the middle is the right size to allow the insertion of four fingers when the object is gripped for striking against a flint, producing sparks to ignite tinder.

A second specimen, purchased from an Oglala woman, is similar except that it is made from a straight piece of iron bent in an oval (fig. 131). It is four and one-half inches long and two inches wide. The ends are curled, and the opening is large enough for the insertion of four fingers. Sulfur matches replaced firesteels on the Plains in the 1860s.

Horse Equipment

The Tetons made comparatively little use of standard horse equipment in the early 1800s. A few bits and bridles were listed in fur company inventories, but they were probably for the use of clerks and white trappers. The Tetons obtained horses at a precontact date and seem to have developed their own styles of rawhide bridles and bits. However, they did purchase bridles and bits later in the nineteenth century. G. P. Beauvais had seventy "fancy Mexican bridle bits" stolen from his trading stock by Miniconjou and Cheyenne Indians in 1865.[35] A fancy Mexican bit from the nineteenth century is

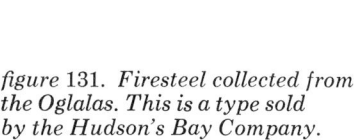

figure 130. Oval firesteel from an 1840 campsite. This was the common trade type. (MFT)

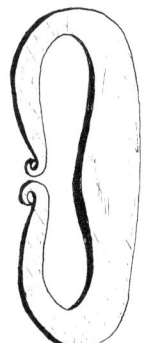

figure 131. Firesteel collected from the Oglalas. This is a type sold by the Hudson's Bay Company. (MFT)

figure 132. Cheek piece of a hand-forged nineteenth-century Mexican bit with silver inlays and engraving. This was purchased from an Oglala. (MFT)

shown in figure 132. It is ornamented with silver and is hand forged. The Tetons manufactured many saddles from elk horn and wood. The native pad saddle, akin to a pillow stuffed with buffalo hair, was hardly suitable for the warpath or rough riding. The arduous task of making a good saddle from native materials caused many Tetons to purchase California or Spanish saddles from traders, and some were given out as annuity items.

In the post–Civil War period, the Tetons purchased or captured army saddles of the McClellan type (at the Custer battle the Tetons stripped the horses of all equipment, including bits, bridles, saddles, and girths). The typical McClellan army saddle of the period was made of wood and iron covered with rawhide. A slot was cut in the middle of the saddle lengthwise to help keep the horse cool in summer and the rider warm in winter. There was no horn, and the cantle or back was low like that of an English saddle. Black leather skirts were attached on each side with brass screws. The stirrups were made of wood and had hoods over the front. One dated 1863 is illustrated in figure 133. Figure 134 shows a McClellan saddle in the Smithsonian Institution. It is believed to have been captured from troops at the Battle of the Little Big Horn. On the left rear portion, behind the cantle, is branded "M 7 C," believed to be a Seventh Cavalry property mark. The saddle, even though it was recaptured from Indians about two weeks after the Custer debacle, has been extensively modified. Virtually all the metal parts have been removed, and even the

figure 133. *McClellan army saddle, marked "Watervliet Arsenal 1863" on the brass shield attached to the pommel. This type, with many variations, was used through the Indian Wars period, and surplus ones were sold in considerable numbers by Indian traders after the Civil War.* (MFT)

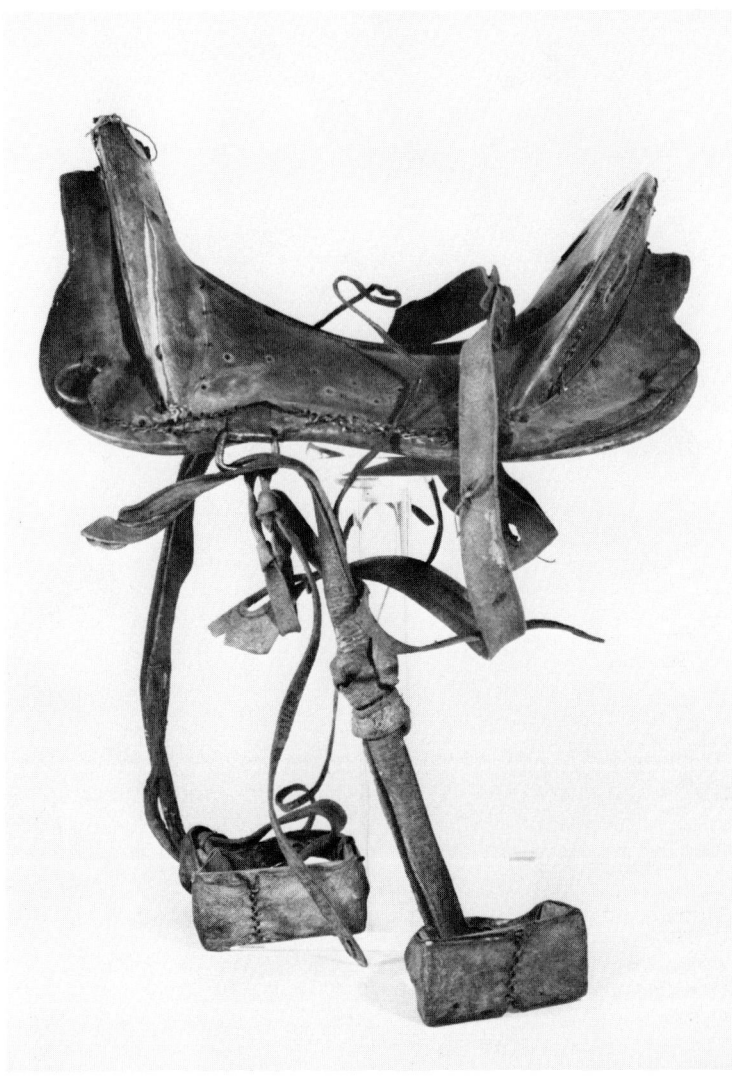

figure 134. *McClellan saddle captured by Tetons at the Custer battle and recaptured by the army a few weeks later. (SI)*

stirrups have been replaced with Indian-made ones of wood. The conventional rigging has been replaced with rawhide.

That the Tetons continued to make saddles after the Civil War is indicated by an order for annuity goods in 1870 to be supplied to the Tetons at Cheyenne River (South Dakota). The agent requested "1,200 Iron rings 3 in. for saddles."[36] These rings were used to attach the girth and stirrups to the saddle proper.

Files

As mentioned previously, files were used by the Tetons in making arrowheads. They were also useful for sharpening axes, hoes, and other heavy tools. Files of various sizes and cut —all of the common types available today—are listed in nineteenth-century traders' inventories. Files were evidently used as metal saws, and gun barrels were frequently filed rather than sawed off. Files were also heated and pressed on wooden handles, stems, and other articles to produce a dark checkered and banded effect which was quite pleasing as a decoration. I have observed no examples of very old files from the Tetons.

Miscellaneous Metal Tools

When civilization pressed the Tetons from all sides, the Indian fur trade as an organized business crumbled into a sporadic and highly dangerous traffic. The Tetons were forced to

figure 135. *Collection of metal objects from the Wounded Knee battlefield. Left to right: plated spoon, table knife, broken butcher knife with very late large copper handle rivets, bone-handled pocket knife, awl made from a knife, butcher knife, Springfield carbine sling snaffle or hook, tin cup handle. (MFT)*

utilize more unusual forms of utensils because of their inability to obtain the standard trade goods they had received in the past.

As a result of massive warfare with the United States Army, the increased sale of Civil War surplus by the few remaining traders, and peace commission gifts of surplus army material, the Teton lodges of 1875 exhibited marked parallels with an army camp. Army coats and hats were in vogue; army pistols, rifles, and saddles supplemented the warriors' needs; and the everyday utensils smacked of an army mess hall.

In 1917, W. M. Camp located the site of the Slim Buttes battle, ninety miles north of Rapid City, South Dakota. There on September 9, 1876, American Horse's Oglala hostiles were surprised by troops under General Anson Mills. The camp was destroyed and all the lodges and their contents burned. The remnants of the battle were picked up by Camp and a crew. The metal articles included three broken iron teakettles; several coffeepots; three galvanized water buckets; tin pans, basins, cups, and cans; a broken butcher knife; iron parts of a saddle tree; arrow points; the top of a canteen; buttons; and numerous iron hooks and handles of five-gallon water kegs.[37] Thus in the post–Civil War period the Teton had begun to replace his bladder water container, his trade kettle, and his elk horn saddle with more civilized equipment. Constant pressure and the proximity of suitable replacements caused him to acculturate further and give up many primitive crafts.

The Wounded Knee massacre of 1890 brought to a close the epic warfare waged against the Tetons. A band of Miniconjous, fearing reprisals for their participation in the Ghost Dance cult, fled from Standing Rock Reservation south to obtain protection from Red Cloud and the Oglalas at Pine Ridge. Caught by regular army troops and Cheyenne scouts, the camp was being disarmed when a gun discharged. Hearing the shot, artillerymen with a battery of Hotchkiss one-inch cannons raked the village, killing dozens of frightened men, women, and children and some of their own comrades. Repeated cavalry charges on the survivors brought the death toll to nearly three hundred. Most of the victims' possessions were lost there, and a number of artifacts were later recovered from the battlefield. The pitiful assortment of tools found indicates the impoverished situation of the Miniconjous at that time.

Most interesting of the tools is a set of eating utensils which may be army issue. The spoon is iron and shows vestiges of nickel plating on the bowl. It is seven inches long and appears to be a typical, cheap spoon such as one might buy today. The knife, ten and one-eighth inches long, has a lead handle, sunken in the center, with a standard table knife blade. Although all marks have corroded away, it is almost certainly an army mess knife.

A scraper or cutting tool of some sort which has been made from a large butcher knife was also found. The blade has been ground off to within two inches of the handle. The letters "ED" (possibly from "warranted") still are visible on the blade. The wood handle is held on with three very large, flat copper rivets. This type of manufacture is uncommon in the nineteenth century. The overall length of the knife is six and one-fourth inches.

A pocket knife is included in the collection, as well as a carbine sling snap. The knife is two-bladed, and has a horn handle. It measures three and one-half inches, with the blades rusted to the case in a closed position. The sling snap was used to hook the ring on the left side of the .45–70 Springfield carbine. It is typical of the thousands of pieces of military supplies which the Tetons must have captured in thirty-five years of warfare. These artifacts are illustrated in figure 135. Other tools and the ornaments found on the Wounded Knee battlefield are described elsewhere in the text.

One can see that by 1890 the material culture of the Tetons had indeed reached a low ebb. The traditional trade goods had nearly vanished. One might believe that the items found at Slim Buttes and Wounded Knee were simply junk salvaged from the cellar of an old farmhouse. The significance of the items lies in their insignificance; no longer would men labor to bring the Tetons specialized goods to please their tastes.

Notes

1. Abel, *Tabeau's Narrative*, p. 180.
2. Erwin N. Thompson, *Fort Union Trading Post* (Washington, D.C.: National Park Service, 1968) pt. 2, p. 147.
3. Marvin C. Ross, *The West of Alfred Jacob Miller* (Norman: University of Oklahoma Press, 1968), p. 79.
4. Catlin, *North American Indians*, 2: 266.
5. Orders Outward, vol. III, Order to Cutler & Stacey, Sheffield, August 31, 1836, p. 148, and Goods Received from Hiram Cutler, November 24, 1836, p. 365, American Fur Company's Papers, New-York Historical Society, New York, N.Y.

6. Russell, *Firearms, Traps, and Tools*, p. 186.
7. Order to Gillespie, Moffat, Finlay and Co., London, November 8, 1827, American Fur Company's Papers, vol. II, Orders Outward, New-York Historical Society, New York, N.Y.
8. *Annual Report of the Commissioner of Indian Affairs, 1870*, pp. 69–70; see also Orders Received, U.S. Bureau of Indian Affairs, Indian Office, Finance Division Contracts and Bonds, Supplies, vol. 2, p. 99, Order to Lamson and Goodnow Mfg. Co., May 24, 1877, RG 75, NARS, and Ronald H. Switzer, "Butcher Knives as Historical Sources," *Museum of the Fur Trade Quarterly* 8, no. 1 (Spring 1972): 5–7.
9. Fort Pierre Letterbook, Honoré Picotte to Alexander Culbertson, June 15, 1836, Missouri Historical Society, Saint Louis, Mo.
10. Henry C. Mercer, *Ancient Carpenter's Tools* (Doylestown, Pa.: Bucks County Historical Society, 1951), p. 7.
11. Peterson, *American Indian Tomahawks*, p. 46.
12. John Francis McDermott, *Seth Eastman* (Norman: University of Oklahoma Press, 1961), pl. 90.
13. *Annual Report of the Commissioner of Indian Affairs, 1870*, p. 70.
14. Clark Wissler, *Indians of the Plains*, Handbook no. 1 (New York: American Museum of Natural History, 1948), pp. 24–26.
15. Maximilian, Alexander Phillip (Prince of Wied-Neuwied), *Travels in the Interior of North America*, vol. 23 of *Early Western Travels, 1748–1846*, ed. Reuben Gold Thwaites (Cleveland: Arthur H. Clark Co., 1906), p. 322.
16. Acting Agent, Cheyenne River Agency, to Commissioner, March 6, 1870, Roll 841, Microcopy No. 234, Letters Received, Office of Indian Affairs, RG 75, NARS.
17. *Annual Report of the Commissioner of Indian Affairs, 1870*, p. 70.
18. Acting Agent, Upper Platte Agency, to Commissioner, May 28, 1870, Letters Received, RG 75, NARS.
19. Fort Pierre Letterbook, James Hamilton to Pratte, Chouteau and Co., Saint Louis, December 10, 1835, Missouri Historical Society, Saint Louis, Mo.
20. Contract Books, Office of Indian Affairs, Book no. 8, pp. 490–92. RG 75, NARS.
21. Ledger Accounts, Chouteau Maffitt Collections, vol. II, p. 26, Missouri Historical Society, Saint Louis, Mo.
22. Frances Densmore, *Teton Sioux Music*, Bulletin 61, Bureau of American Ethnology (Washington, D.C.: G.P.O., 1918), p. 438.
23. D. R. Risley, Whetstone Agency, to Commissioner, March 8, 1873, Letters Received, Whetstone Agency, 1873, RG 75, NARS.
24. Maximilian, *Travels*, p. 309.
25. Ernest Thompson Seton, *Lives of Game Animals*, 8 vols. (New York: Doubleday, Doran, and Co., 1929), vol. 3, pt. 2, p. 535.
26. The Engagés, "Indian Awls," *Museum of the Fur Trade Quarterly*, 7, no. 2 (Summer 1971): 2–3.
27. Seton, *Lives of Game Animals*, vol. 3, pt. 1, p. 11.
28. The use of scythe blades by the Tetons in tanning is described in E. M. Flannery, *Aboriginal Methods of Skin Dressing*, (New York: American Museum of Natural History, 1909), p. 309.
29. "A Day at the Birmingham Factories," *Penny Magazine* (London), n.s. 13 (1844): 507.
30. Orders Outward, American Fur Company's Papers, vol. II, New-York State Historical Society, New York, N.Y.
31. Robert W. Neuman, "Porcupine Quill Flatteners from the

Central United States," *American Antiquity* 26, no. 1 (1960): 99.
32. Voucher to Bramble & Miner, Yankton, South Dakota, April 17, 1871, Letters Received, Whetstone Agency, 1871–72, RG 75, NARS.
33. Russell, *Firearms, Traps, and Tools*, p. 352.
34. For basic types of firesteels, see the Engagés, "Trade Fire Steels," *Museum of the Fur Trade Quarterly* 7, no. 4 (Winter 1971): 2–4.
35. G. P. Beauvais vs. Minniconjou and Northern Cheyenne Indians, Claim no. 7099 for depredations occurring on February 15, 1865, Records of the United States Court of Claims, RG 123 and 205, NARS.
36. "List of Annuity Goods Required for Grand River Agency for 1870," Letters Received, Upper Platte Agency, 1870, RG 75, NARS.
37. W. M. Camp, "Discovery of the Lost Site of the Slim Buttes Battle," *South Dakota Historical Collections* 9 (1918): 55–68.

Chapter Five

Metal Ornaments

While every Indian tribe showed strong affinities for decoration and ornamentation, the Tetons were characteristically plain in their costuming habits. They seem generally to have preferred more utilitarian goods when compared with other Plains Indians such as the Kiowas and Cheyennes, who displayed much greater extravagances of ornamentation. The Tetons did, however, acquire ornaments from both the Southwest and Missouri River trade routes, thus giving their decorative effects a bicultural flavor. After the Civil War, great masses of geometric beadwork were popular among the Tetons.

The Teton Dakotas were probably acquainted with the standard eastern ornaments from British and American traders. Edwin T. Denig, writing of the period before 1854, remarked that the Sioux generally preferred silver ornaments like arm and wrist bands, headbands, "gorgets, brooches, ear wheels, finger rings, and ear bobs,"[1] although this does not agree with other sources. Perhaps Denig was referring to the Eastern or Middle Sioux, who were more like the Woodland tribes in dress style. Denig himself lists only brass ornaments when describing typical Sioux costumes. In 1831–32, the Fort Union inventory showed silver gorgets, "silver hat crowns," and two sizes each of silver arm and wrist bands for sale.[2] At least one silver gorget has been collected from the Sioux, and a number of silver ornaments have been found in Arikara sites.

Silver ornaments like those popular in the east enjoyed some vogue among the Plains tribes, but that popularity evidently did not last past the 1830s. The Tetons did not attach great importance to silver or gold as did eastern tribes, and soon traders brought them ornaments of brass which could be sold at a much lower price and higher profit. Brass ornaments were characteristic of the Tetons until reservation days. By 1860, a nonferrous alloy of copper, nickel, and zinc, known as German silver, was being used to manufacture ornaments such as rings, crosses, pectorals, arm bands, and belt disks. The Tetons also purchased sheets of German silver and made some of these ornaments themselves. For comparative purposes, silver, items mentioned by Denig are shown in figure 136.

Earbobs and Dangles

The earbob was a standard decoration among all the Indian tribes east of the Rocky Mountains, and is very common in colonial Woodland sites. The Tetons purchased them in large numbers. The Fort Union inventory for 1850 lists fifty pairs of silver earbobs.[3] Silver ornaments were not typical trade goods on the plains, but silver earbobs from the Tetons are common. The earbobs excavated at Teton sites or collected from the Tetons are typically either brass or silver. A brass specimen excavated at a Teton site of the 1830s is shown in figure 137. It is made of a round ball with a brass wire through it by which it is suspended from a perforation in the ear. A cone-shaped dangle hangs from a ring soldered to the lower side of the ball. Earbobs were found at the Wounded Knee battlefield, indicating that their period of usage covered the greater part of the nineteenth century. Frequently, clusters of earbobs were hung from the top to the lobe of the ear.

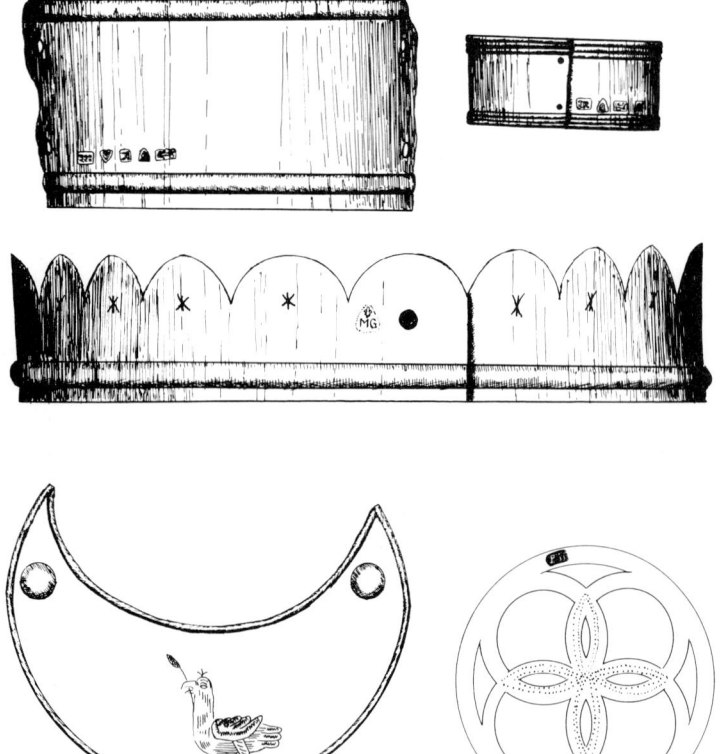

figure 136. Silver trade ornaments. From the top, left to right: arm band, wrist band, headband, gorget, ear wheel, and brooch. (MFT)

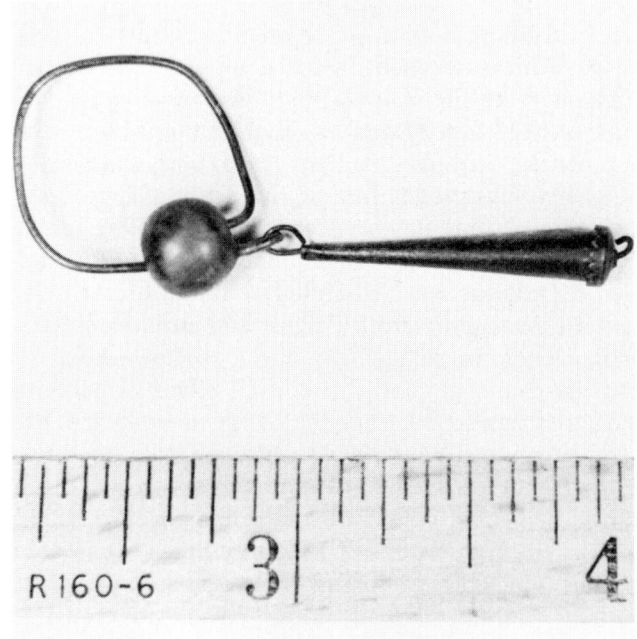

figure 137. Brass earbob from a Teton campsite, period 1830. (MFT)

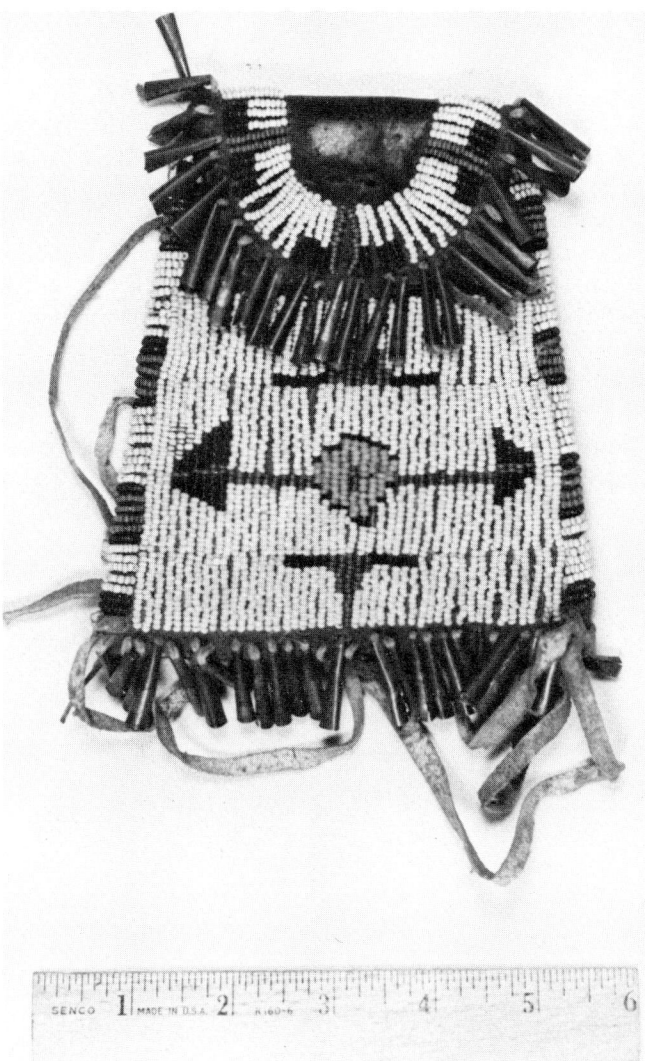

figure 138. *Pouch for carrying flint, firesteel, and tinder. The heavy tin dangle decoration is typical of the period 1860–80 and later. (KOL)*

John Choloff, who worked in a reservation store at Pine Ridge in 1897–98, remembered that they sold earbobs at that time which were similar to the one illustrated. These came from S. A. Frost and Son in New York. Choloff said that they were out of fashion by about 1910.[4]

Dangles were small cone-shaped tin or brass ornaments hung from clothing and containers. They were placed close together along seams so that they produced a tinkling sound when moved. I believe that most dangles were made from tin cans by the Tetons themselves; no references were found to the sale of them. They are generally irregular in shape, sometimes as long as two inches, and made of thin iron. They have been observed on Teton costumes in the period 1850–80, and some copper dangles were found at the Wounded Knee battlefield. In addition, several dangles made by drilling a hole through the end of a thimble were seen. A pouch with dangles is illustrated in figure 138. In the early nineteenth century, the Plains Indians used hooves and dewclaws to achieve the same effect. Costumes brought back from the Upper Missouri by Lewis and Clark have dangles on them, so the Tetons surely had access to them by the time of that expedition.

Rings

Rings were generally made of brass for the Teton trade, although a few were made of lead and in the last half of the nineteenth century, some German silver rings were worn by

figure 139. *Lead ring from a campsite, about 1840. (MFT)*

figure 140. *Brass ring from an 1840 campsite. (MFT)*

the Tetons. Figure 139 shows a ring from an 1840 village site in Nebraska. It is made from a flat strip of lead, the two ends of which are not joined together, and has parallel lines around the circumference. It is probably of Indian manufacture.

Figure 140 depicts a common brass ring. This specimen, one and eight-tenths inches thick, was found at the same site as the ring described above. Norman Feder believes that "by 1805 . . . brass finger rings must have been available on the Plains."[5] Sir Richard Burton commented that the Tetons at Fort Laramie had their "finger[s] . . . after an African fashion, adorned with the same [brass] metals, which the savage ever prefers to the gold or silver."[6]

The German silver rings collected from the Teton Dakotas are generally quite modern in styling. One specimen of this type, shown in Figure 141, was obtained from Young-Man-Afraid-of-His-Horse, an Oglala, about 1890. The finger band is one-fourth inch wide and one inch long, and is stamped with scallops, circles, and triangles. This ring was accessioned into the Smithsonian Anthropology collections in 1901.

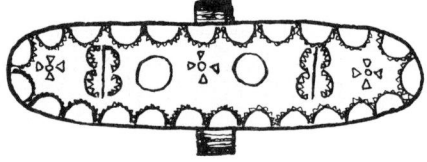

figure 141. *German silver ring which belonged to Young-Man-Afraid-of-His-Horse. (SI)*

figure 142. *Hank of cut steel beads from a trader's unsold stock, period 1890. The original tag,* "MADE IN FRANCE," *is not shown. (MFT)*

Beads

The so-called cut steel beads carried on many trading company inventories were frequently not metal at all, but were iridescent glass which resembled polished metal. Some beads were made of cut or faceted steel, and are quite small, but the most common metal beads used by the Tetons were brass. Thousands of them have been found at Teton sites of the post–Civil War period; over three thousand were found at one site in western South Dakota. These beads are shown clearly in

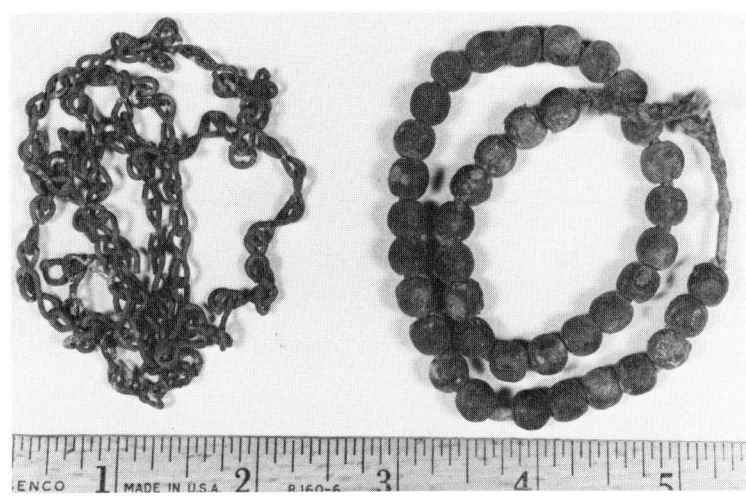

figure 143. *Brass chain and beads found at Wounded Knee. (MFT)*

figure 144. *Photograph of Short Bull showing brass beads at the top of his breast plate and brass beads threaded on a lock of his hair. (SI)*

many photographs of Teton Dakotas. They are round and average one-fourth inch in diameter. Both the cut steel and the brass beads were probably manufactured in France. I have seen an original hank of the cut beads with French labels attached, and the brass beads were called "French beads" in trading inventories. A hank of cut steel beads and a string of brass beads are shown in figures 142 and 143. The use of brass beads is shown in figure 144.

Bells

Figures 145–150 illustrate the types of bells sold to the Tetons. Figure 145 depicts a cast brass bell, period 1800. Figure 146 shows a brass bell with a copper rivet for attachment to harness, period 1860, that was found at a Teton campsite. The cast brass bell depicted in figure 147 is from a Teton campsite near the Platte River and has a nineteenth-century provenience. Figure 148 shows large iron bells, circa 1880, from a Teton grass dance outfit.

The specimen labeled figure 149 is typical of the bells sold to the Tetons in the nineteenth century. The Fort Union inventories list 112 gross of hawk bells in 1851.[7] These bells are found on Teton costumes throughout the nineteenth century, and I observed numerous examples on clothing and from archaeological investigations. Their name is probably derived from their use in falconry. They are small, round bells with flattened ends and a wire loop for attachment at the top.

figure 145. *Cast brass bell from before 1800. The attachment loop is an integral part of the casting. (MFT)*

figure 146. *Brass bell with copper rivet for attachment. (MFT)*

figure 147. *Heavy cast brass bell of the nineteenth century. (MFT)*

figure 148. *Anklet with large iron bells, about 1880. (MFT)*

Figure 150 shows two Oglalas, Black Elk and Elk, about 1880. Two types of bells, one of which is bell-shaped with clappers, can be seen on their costumes.

figure 149. *Brass hawk bells. The wire loop for attachment can be seen on the specimen at right. (MFT)*

figure 150. *Black Elk and Elk, with various types of bells on their costumes. (SI)*

Arm Bands and Bracelets

As previously mentioned, the Tetons probably bought silver wrist and arm bands from traders, but these went out of fashion and bracelets of other metals were substituted. Matt Field in 1844 met a Western Dakota near Fort Laramie who was wearing arm bands made out of two old iron trunk handles.[8] Brass arm bands were popular in the latter half of the nineteenth century, and the tribes around the Tetons wore them extensively. Only a few are known to have come from the Tetons, however. I have examined several pairs of ribbed and plain brass bands, in widths from two to five inches, all of which were made from flat brass strips bent in a circle. One pair of German silver arm bands, shown in figure 151, was re-

figure 152. *Ribbed brass arm band from Wounded Knee. (MFT)*

figure 151. *German silver adjustable arm bands with professionally engraved designs. (MFT)*

cently collected from the Oglalas. They are three-fourths inch wide and twelve inches in circumference. The bands are adjustable by means of an ingenious hook at one end and a series of holes into which the hook is fastened at the other end of the strip. They are engraved along the borders and have peculiar oval designs running lengthwise in the middle. These arm bands appear to be commercially made and are almost identical to an arm band collected from a Menominee Indian in Wisconsin.[9]

A pair of very narrow commercial arm bands were collected from a Teton in Montana by a minister and are now in

83

figure 153. *Engraved nickel-plated brass bracelet from Wounded Knee. (MFT)*

figure 154. *Arm band fragment from Wounded Knee. It is nickel-plated brass with a checkered design rolled into the surface. (MFT)*

the Smithsonian's collections. These are nickel-plated brass, five-eighths inch wide, and have a rolled Greek key design the length of them. A single arm band, collected from the Oglalas in the 1870s, is German silver. It is two inches wide and ten inches long, and is engraved in the Indian style with a rocker tool, but is quite professional in appearance. The center motif is a full-face buffalo head, with geometric designs on either side.

Bracelets for women are more common, but again they appear to have been especially popular among the Tetons only in the period 1850–1900. I have noted plain and ribbed bracelets of brass, German silver, and copper, and a few of nickel-plated brass, from the Tetons. Arm bands and portions of bracelets found at Wounded Knee are shown in figures 152, 153, and 154. They are all similar, with simple but professional-looking engraving. The most common women's bracelets are those made of brass wire, the use of which is discussed below.

Lead

Lead was a common trade item obviously dating back to the first shipments of guns received by the Tetons. It is included in this study because of its use in the ornamentation of pipe bowls.

Maximilian states that "the pipes of the Dakotas are very beautiful; in truth, the most beautiful of all North American

figure 155. Red Shirt with lead-inlaid pipe. (SI)

Indians."[10] Bodmer made several paintings of pipes inlaid with concentric lead rings; an excellent one is shown in the *Atlas* of his works.[11] I have observed this inlay work as it is done by the Tetons. Grooves are cut in the stone, and the grooved area is wrapped with rawhide. An opening is left in the top, into which molten lead is poured. Then the rawhide is removed and the lead is filed smooth with the surface of the stone. Figure 155 is a photograph of a Teton with a splendid inlaid pipe.

A second use of lead, not for ornamental purposes, was in weapon making. Knife clubs, described above, frequently have had lead poured around the blades to hold them firmly in place.

Peace Medals

Peace medals were given or sold to Indians of nearly every tribe as symbols of prestige and authority. They were distributed by both Spanish and British emissaries to the Tetons around the beginning of the nineteenth century,[12] although I could locate no known British or Spanish medals from the Tetons. By inference, it is assumed that the British medals bore the bust of King George III on the obverse with his arms and supporters on the reverse. These were frequently listed as presents for Indians to be shipped to Mackinac on the Great Lakes.[13] A photograph of a Dakota, probably a Teton, wearing one of these British medals, is shown in figure 156.

figure 156. *Teton wearing a British peace medal (below) and an American medal with the bust of President Grant (above). (SI)*

There is little information on what the Spanish medals looked like. A peace medal made of an engraved circle with a silver pillar dollar bearing Charles IV's bust soldered in the center was found at a Pawnee site in Nebraska. This medal, now in the Nebraska State Historical Society collections at Lincoln, might be similar to the type given to the Tetons. It may have been one of those handed out by Lieutenant Don Facundo Malgares of the Spanish garrison at Santa Fe just prior to Pike's visit in 1806. The Spanish government in Saint Louis had better trade routes to Europe than did the isolated New Mexicans, and the Spanish medals seen by Lewis and Clark could have been brought from Spain. A struck medal from the Spanish was found at Prairie du Chien, Wisconsin, in 1864. It is a silver military service medal, with a bust of the king and the legend "CAROLUS III REY DE ESPANA E DE LAS INDIAS" on the obverse. The reverse shows a wreath with the inscription "POR MERITO." The medal has a suspension loop, and is two and one-half inches in diameter.[14]

The United States issued medals to the Tetons in 1804. They were made of thin silver shells held together with a ring around the circumference. This is the only shell medal issued by the government. The obverse bears a bust of Thomas Jefferson with the motto "TH. JEFFERSON PRESIDENT OF THE U.S. A.D. 1801." Figure 157 shows the reverse of this medal, which carries a crossed hatchet and pipe, two hands clasped in a handshake, and the motto "PEACE AND FRIENDSHIP."[15]

This was the first in the series of Indian peace medals

figure 157. *Reverse of a Jefferson peace medal.*

which were struck until Benjamin Harrison's term of office. The most common medals received by the Tetons were those issued during the terms of office of John Quincy Adams, Andrew Johnson, and Ulysses S. Grant, although any presidential medal could have been issued to them. The Adams medals are similar to the Jefferson ones except that they were solid silver. The Johnson medal bears a different reverse (fig. 158).

It depicts an Indian shaking hands with an allegorical representation of liberty. In the background is a bust of George Washington. All of the American medals described above were minted in two-, two-and-one-half-, and three-inch diameters. The style of the Grant medal was changed from that of the earlier medals. It bears Grant's bust on the obverse with the mottos "UNITED STATES OF AMERICA," "LIBERTY JUSTICE AND EQUALITY," and "LET US HAVE PEACE." On the reverse is a globe and a Bible, with various agricultural implements in the background. Around the edge are thirty-six stars with the motto "ON EARTH PEACE GOOD WILL TOWARD MEN, 1871." These Grant medals were silver and were issued only in the two-and-one-half-inch size.[16]

Some traders also issued medals to the Tetons; specimens have been found which come from three basic sources. The American Fur Company's northern subsidiary, the Upper Missouri Outfit, issued silver medals in the period 1833–44. These bear the portrait of John Jacob Astor on the obverse with the title "PRESIDENT OF THE AMERICAN FUR COMPANY." On the back are two sets of crossed pipes and two clasped hands, with the wording "FORT UNION U.M.O. PEACE AND FRIENDSHIP." These were issued in the two-and-one-half- and three-inch sizes.[17] When Pierre Chouteau, Jr., acquired the Upper Missouri Outfit in 1834, he issued a large four-inch shell medal in copper or white metal made in the same manner as the Jefferson medals.[18] The bust of Pierre Chouteau, Jr., and the words "PIERRE CHOUTEAU JR. & CO. * UPPER MISSOURI OUTFIT" are on the obverse, with the clasped hands, pipe and tomahawk, and "PEACE

figure 158. *Reverse of a silver Andrew Johnson government peace medal. (MFT)*

figure 159. *Obverse and reverse of the Pierre Chouteau, Jr., and Company Upper Missouri Outfit medal issued about 1834. (MFT)*

AND FRIENDSHIP" on the back. The specimens I observed are dated 1834 or 1844 on the reverse. Both sides are shown in figure 159. A third type of trader's medal has been observed among the Tetons. It bears a three-quarters view of Washington on the obverse with the words "GEORGE WASHINGTON THE FATHER OF HIS COUNTRY * 1789." The reverse bears the usual pipe and tomahawk and hands with an oak wreath and the motto "FRIENDSHIP – THE – PIPE OF PEACE." Bauman Belden states they were first minted around 1845,[19] but one was found in the ruins of a Pawnee village in Nebraska which was destroyed in 1844. Lt. G. K. Warren obtained one from the Tetons in the 1850s. My father notes that these medals were still

figure 160. *Obverse of the Washington trader's medal. This specimen is pewter. (MFT)*

figure 161. *Reverse of the Washington trader's medal. (MFT)*

figure 162. *Tetons wearing peculiar stamped sheet brass medals. (SI)*

being struck in 1938. Specimens have been reported in pewter, aluminum, bronze, silver, and German silver.[20] A pewter example collected from the Oglalas is shown in figures 160 and 161. What may be the last type of medal made for the Indians can be seen in figure 162. This photograph, taken in 1913, shows two Oglalas wearing stamped brass medallions which were issued by the Miller 101 Ranch Wild West Show to their performers.

Brass Tacks

Brass tacks used by the Tetons in the nineteenth century were common furniture tacks of the period. The head and shank are cast in one piece, and the shank is square. The tacks were used as ornaments on belts, knife sheaths, war clubs, gunstocks, and other objects. Today many fake Indian items are brass tacked to lend authenticity, but modern tacks have a round steel shank. Brass tacks were available to the Tetons before 1835[21] and were used by them in great profusion after 1850. The annuity goods given to the Tetons in 1878 included 166 papers of brass tacks.[22] A tacked knife sheath from Wounded Knee and a solid brass tack are shown in figure 163, and figure 81 depicts a Teton girl wearing a tacked belt.

Pectorals and Crosses

The large crescent-shaped silver trade and military gorgets or neck ornaments supplied to Indians by agents and traders in the eastern United States did not seem to find much popularity on the plains. Some have been found on the Upper Missouri, but they are quite scarce. One interesting reference is made to "twenty brass and 20 tin gorgets" at Fort Union in 1850, and Denig made a cryptic reference to "brass breastplates" worn by the Sioux.[23] An example of these could not be found, but at least the references indicate that silver ornaments were no longer in vogue, probably because of the Plains Indians' ready acceptance of base metal ornaments.

The pectoral, worn extensively by the Kiowas and Cheyennes and to a lesser degree by the Tetons, did not evolve from the eastern trade gorget but instead came from the Southwest. Rosemary Ellison states that: "Mexican silversmiths were itinerant craftsmen who . . . geared their work to the wishes of the Plains tribesmen. They introduced massive, solid pieces such as breastplates and crosses. . . . The crosses were undoubtedly copied from silver examples seen gracing the altars of Catholic missions."[24]

Pectorals generally fit the following description. They are made of German silver, roughly triangular in shape with scalloped edges on two sides. The triangle, appearing to be a

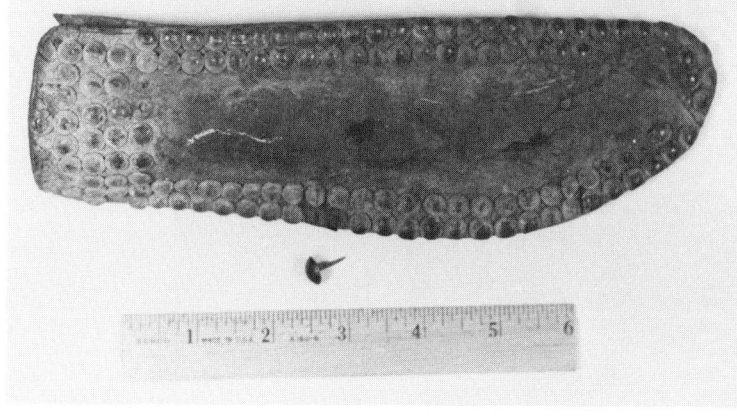

figure 163. *Knife sheath decorated with brass tacks, probably Miniconjou, from the Wounded Knee battlefield. Below it is a nineteenth-century brass tack. (MFT)*

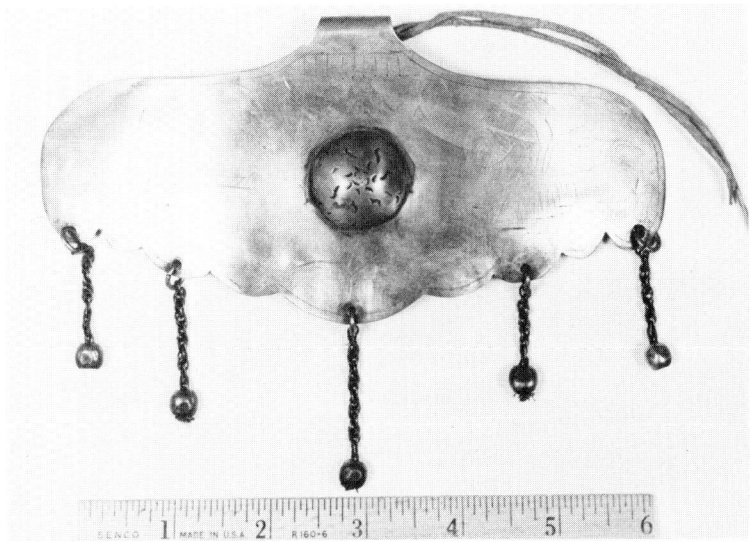

figure 164. *Pectoral made of German silver showing Indian workmanship. (MFT)*

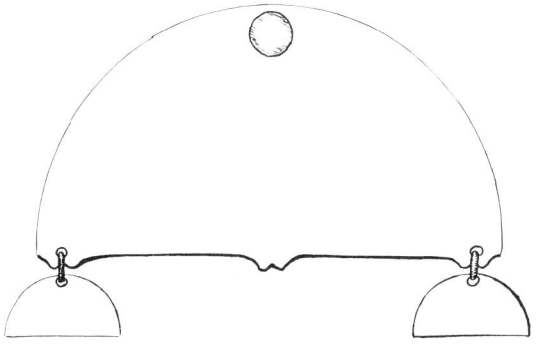

figure 165. *Pectoral worn by White Eyes, from a photograph.*

figure 166. *Aberrant form of pectoral, collected in Montana. (SI)*

representation of a cloud, is suspended from the neck with one point down. In the center of the uppermost side are holes or a curled piece of metal for suspension. German silver crescents or chains are generally attached at the points of the triangle. A splendid example obtained from the Tetons is shown in figure 164. It is crudely engraved with an Indian on horseback, a man, and a cross. A round boss is soldered in the center, and five pieces of silver chain with silver balls on the ends are attached to holes in the lower edge. The piece has a curled edge which serves as a suspension loop.

Records of pectorals are to be found in both photographs and pictographs. Photographs show two pectorals worn by Good Buffalo and Thigh, Oglala warriors.[25] They are similar, but one has three crescents suspended from it, while the other has only one large crescent. Both pectorals hang from handkerchiefs around the Indians' necks. An Oglala pictograph census roster from 1878 shows Black Bear wearing a pectoral attached to a pipebone breastplate.[26]

The shapes of pectorals vary a great deal from the standard "cloud" shape. White Eyes, an Oglala, wore a semicircular pectoral, which is sketched in figure 165 from an 1872 photograph. Another aberrant example is shown in figure 166. Collected from the Tetons at Poplar River, Montana, before 1894 and now in the Smithsonian's Anthropology collections, it is German silver and is Indian made. The shape is reminiscent of a woman's dress, with a human figure hanging at the bottom. There are rocker-engraved decorations on it: some random lines on the figure, four human heads along the lower edge, and parts of what may be a horse on the upper part. Brass has been used to plug part of the suspension hole.

Crosses of German silver are more typical of the Tetons than are pectorals. In the same 1878 Oglala roster that shows one pectoral, four warriors—Little Hawk, Iron Crow, Long Dog, and Iron Hawk—are depicted wearing crosses.[27] An excellent photograph (fig. 167) of the Oglala chief Young-Man-Afraid-of-His-Horse shows a beautiful, large cross. Figure 168 is an example of a cross obtained from the Tetons. It belonged to No Flesh, an Oglala, and appears to be Indian made and is of nickel-plated brass. A rectangle has been cut out of each horizontal arm of the cross, and crescents are suspended from

figure 167. *Young-Man-Afraid-of-His-Horse, an Oglala chief. A large cross hangs on his chest, and large wire earrings with chain dangles can be clearly seen. (SI)*

figure 168. *Beautiful cross made of nickel-plated brass, from the Oglalas. (MFT)*

the bottom and the arms. Very few crosses of this sort appear to be mass produced, although most seem to have been made by someone fairly professional in metalworking. Other types of crosses, associated with the work of missionaries, are discussed under "Religious Objects."

Hairplates

Hairplates are a distinctive Plains Indian ornament. They became popular around the beginning of the nineteenth century, and I found no examples after 1868. Their use among the Brules was noted by Maximilian. "These Indians let their hair grow long . . . which is ornamented with round pieces."[28] In 1837 Miller painted a picture of Fort Laramie showing in the foreground several Tetons, two of whom have strings of hairplates down their backs (fig. 169). Francis Parkman, at Fort Laramie in 1846, described the use of hairplates by a Dakota: "From the back of his head descended a line of glittering brass plates, tapering from the size of a doubloon to that of a half-dime, a cumbrous ornament, in high vogue among the Dahcotahs, and for which they pay the traders an extravagant price."[29] Sir Richard Burton mentioned hairplates among the Tetons at Fort Laramie in 1860.[30]

Feder, who indexed references to hairplates in the literature, found that they are mentioned among the Tetons from 1808 to 1858.[31] Some of these were brass, some silver, and still others German silver. They were worn singly or in strings of graduated sizes, and all are pierced so that they can be tied to the hair or to a cloth or leather strip. Some are simply engraved and others are plain. Figure 170 depicts a massive hairplate set collected from the Oglalas. Two photographs taken by William Gardiner at Fort Laramie in 1868 show large hairplate sets and also a set of miniature hairplates, which were

figure 169. Alfred Jacob Miller's painting of Tetons at Fort Laramie. Two Indians are clearly wearing hairplates. (Thomas Gilcrease Institute of American History and Art, Tulsa, Oklahoma)

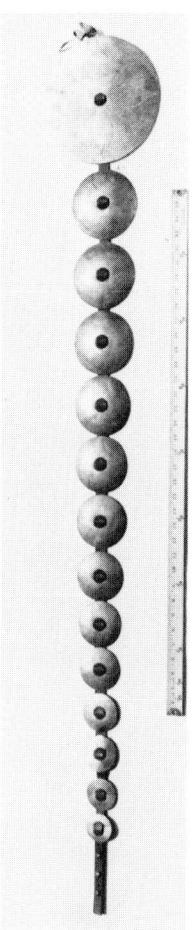

figure 170. Set of brass hairplates from the Oglalas, period 1850–70. (MFT)

figure 171. Photograph by William Gardiner at Fort Laramie in 1868. Running Water at the left is wearing a large set of hairplates. The unidentified Teton at the right is wearing miniature set. An interesting collection of kettles is in the foreground. (NARS)

figure 172. Tetons at Laramie, 1868. The man at extreme left has a string of hairplates wrapped over his shoulder. Note also the "George Washington" hatchet. (SI)

figure 173. Set of miniature hairplates. (MFT)

in vogue among young Plains Indian dandies after the Civil War (figs. 171 and 172). Figure 173 shows a miniature hairplate set.

Belt Disks and Drops

Belt disks were fashionable in the period after the Civil War. Perhaps the use of hairplates was discouraged among the Teton warriors around that time because the belt disk, worn by women, resembled it closely. Examples have been observed made of German silver and nickel-plated brass. They were plain or engraved, with a small eye soldered on the back for attachment. Usually they are convex. The disks were sewn in rows on a wide leather belt, and a row of graduated disks hung from the hip to the ground. An excellent photograph of such a conch belt being worn is figure 174. Charles E. Han-

figure 174. *A Teton woman wearing a conch belt. Note the Niobrara cross worn by the man. (MFT)*

son, Jr., says that Ray Lyons, the Indian trader from Clinton, Nebraska, obtained his stock of belt disks from Germany. Figure 175 shows a belt obtained from the Oglalas and figure 176 an engraved belt disk found at Wounded Knee.

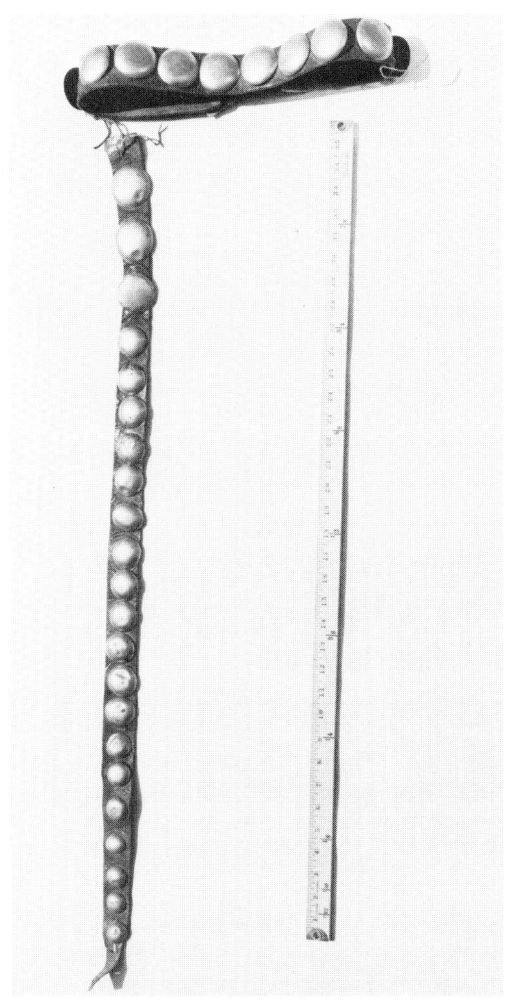

figure 175. *Belt decorated with German silver disks. Collected at Pine Ridge, South Dakota. (MFT)*

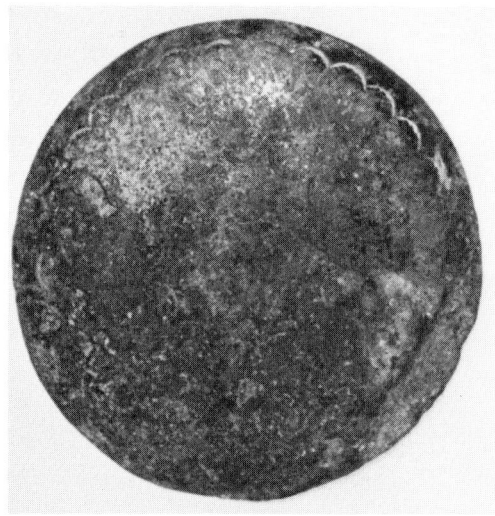

figure 176. *Belt disk found at Wounded Knee. (MFT)*

Chain and Wire

Brass chain was used by the Tetons to a limited extent, and was popular after the Civil War. Generally it was hung in long loops from the ears. Young-Man-Afraid-of-His-Horse wore this style of chain earrings (fig. 167), and several pieces of brass chain were found at the Wounded Knee site mentioned previously (a piece from that site is shown in figure 143).

Brass wire was much more common among the Tetons. Tabeau, in 1805, commented that both the Brule men and women wore "rolls" (circles?) of brass wire in their ears.[32] These brass loop earrings remained popular throughout the nineteenth century. Usually some beads were strung on the

figure 177. *Pawnee Killer, wearing brass loop earrings. Note ring and short-bowled tomahawk. (SI)*

figure 178. *Brass wire bracelets from Wounded Knee. (MFT)*

loop, and frequently chain, bone hairpipes, and beads were hung as pendants from the loops. Figure 177 is a photograph of an Oglala wearing brass wire earrings.

Burton mentions the extensive use of brass wire among the Tetons in 1860 by both men and women for arm bands, earrings, and bracelets.[33] It was an important ornament; G. P. Beauvais had "16 lbs. fine brass wire @ $2 per lb." on hand in 1865, and 250 pounds were included in annuity payments to the Tetons in 1868.[34] Bracelets made of brass wire are continually being found at campsites. Generally, they are simply a piece of brass wire bent in a circle. They are not, as some believe, made of telegraph wire, which is copper. Two Miniconjou

figure 179. *Teton woman wearing a mass of brass wire bracelets. (SI)*

bracelets are shown in figure 178. Figure 179 shows a Teton woman who is wearing dozens of brass wire bracelets.

Iron wire was used for the same type of ornaments as brass wire, and is usually found listed in inventories and annuity lists with brass wire. It was frequently utilized to repair broken club handles, gunstocks, and other weapons. As a decoration, it was wrapped solidly around tomahawk, lance, and knife club handles. Brass wire was sometimes used in this way, but iron wire decorations are more common.

Religious Objects

The missionaries of the nineteenth century found the Indian an excellent subject for their proselytizing, and several Catholic and Episcopal priests worked among the Teton Dakotas. A Catholic medal is illustrated in figures 180 and 181. It was originally attached to a Teton war bundle. Crudely made, it has on the obverse a representation of the Virgin Mary, the date 1830, and the motto "O MARY CONCEIVED WITHOUT SIN PRAY FOR US WHO HAVE RECOURSE TO YOU" in two lines. On the reverse are twelve stars, a cross with an "M" intertwined at the base, and two hearts, one impaled by a sword, and the other with a crown of thorns. An identical specimen was found at Fort John near Scottsbluff, Nebraska.[35]

The Catholic crucifix depicted in figure 182 was collected

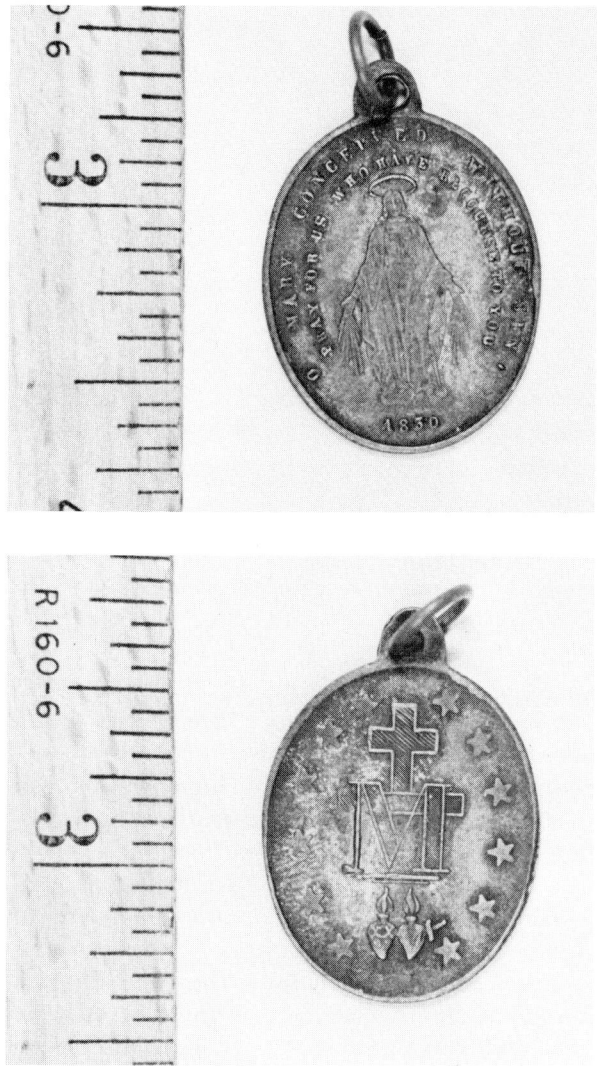

figure 180. *Catholic Immaculate Conception medal from an Indian war bundle. (MFT)*

figure 181. *Reverse of the medal shown in figure 180. (MFT)*

from an Oglala, who stated that it was given to his grandfather about 1880. It is of cast pewter with a brass figure of Christ attached to the cross with three small brass nails. These crucifixes were worn by Tetons as ornaments. Photographs in the Smithsonian of two Sans Arcs show this type of decoration. One was made of an unidentified metal which was cast to imitate two split logs nailed together, with the flat side against the wearer's chest. The bark, knots, and ax-pointed ends are clearly visible. The estimated dimensions for this cross are ten inches long and six inches wide. Long Dog (fig. 183) wore a crucifix much like the one shown in figure 182. He is also holding a knife club. A religious cross worn by Sitting Bull is shown in figure 184. It is drawn from a photograph.

Figure 185 shows an Episcopal "Niobrara" cross, which supposedly was issued in 1878 to new converts among the Tetons. It is nickel-plated brass and bears a Greek legend with four tipis surmounted by crosses at the intersections of arms. Figure 186 is a photograph of Lieutenant Bullhead, who was killed in 1890 during the attempt to arrest Sitting Bull. His Niobrara cross can be seen clearly on his watch fob.

The small brass crucifix illustrated in figure 187 is one which was given to the Sioux at Fort Yates, North Dakota, in the late 1800s. Another Catholic medal of prime significance is shown in figures 188 and 189. It is reported to have been given out around the middle of the nineteenth century by Father Pierre-Jean De Smet. This was obtained at Fort Yates, North Dakota.

figure 182. Large pewter crucifix with brass figure. (MFT)

figure 184. *Crucifix worn by Sitting Bull. (SI)*

figure 183. *Long Dog wearing a crucifix. (SI)*

figure 185. *Nickel-plated brass cross with four tipis surmounted by crosses. This is the Episcopalian Niobrara cross first given out in 1878 to converts. (MFT)*

figure 186. *Lieutenant Bullhead wearing a Niobrara cross, apparently as a watch fob. (SI)*

figure 187. *A small brass crucifix given out by one Father Jerome at Fort Yates, North Dakota, about 1880. (KOL)*

Buttons

A variety of buttons were obtained by the Tetons in the nineteenth century. Garments brought from the Mandans by Lewis and Clark have several sizes of flat brass buttons sewn to them in rows for decoration. Most of the metal buttons were brass. Some are listed in trade goods inventories, specifically ball or bullet buttons and circular flat buttons.[36] The Tetons also obtained military buttons through warfare or annuity payments. Several of these were found at a Teton campsite near Fort Robinson, Nebraska. They bear a United States eagle on the front with the letter *C* on its chest. On the back of each is an eye for attachment and the stamping "G. Horstmann Philada." A collection of buttons from this campsite is shown in figure 190.

figure 188. *Catholic "miraculous" medal believed to have been given out by Father DeSmet. It was identified as one struck in the early nineteenth century by the Jesuits. The figure on the medal is Saint Francis Xavier, founder of that order. (KOL)*

figure 189. *Reverse of the DeSmet medal. (KOL)*

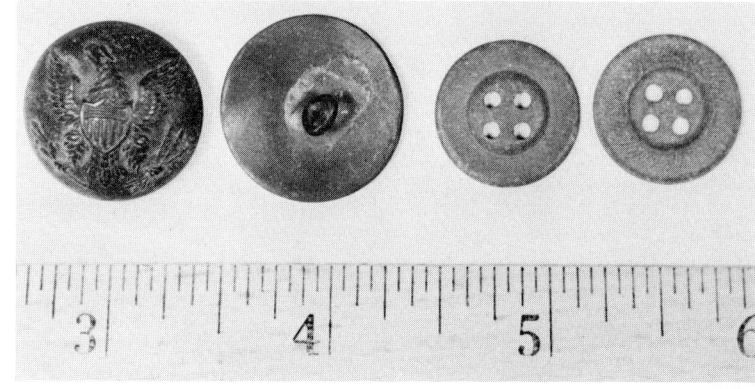

figure 190. *Four buttons from a Teton campsite near Fort Robinson, Nebraska, about 1875. (MFT)*

figure 191. *White Thunder wearing a breastplate made of German silver. (SI)*

Miscellaneous German Silver Ornaments

Hairpipe breastplates became fashionable on the plains in the 1850s. The long beads were first made of shell, and later of cattle bone. However, at least one well-dressed Teton warrior chose to wear a breastplate made of metal beads. White Thunder, a Brule, is shown in figure 191; his breastplate is evidently German silver.

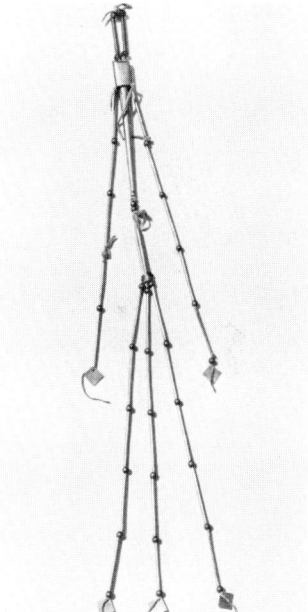

figure 192. *German silver awl case. (MFT)*

Figure 192 shows an awl case collected from the Hunkpapas. The long dangles are German silver tubing sawed into short lengths, with brass beads between them. Small squares of German silver hang at the bottom. Awl cases of this type are not very common and are probably quite late. This example has been converted into a belt drop. Two brass beads have been added at the top, and the awl case cap cannot now be opened.

Southwestern Indians adopted the Mexican-style silver-mounted bridle. A very few of these have come from the Sioux. One from the Museum of the American Indian / Heye Foundation is shown in figure 193.

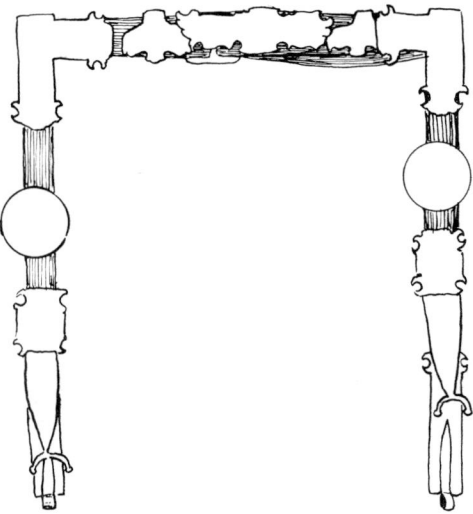

figure 193. *Hunkpapa German silver bridle constructed on the Mexican pattern. (MAI)*

Indian Police Uniforms

An original Indian Police jacket and belt are shown in figure 194. These were obtained on Standing Rock Reservation and were worn by Fool Bear, a Hunkpapa. The buttons are of three types, one of which is the early twentieth-century spread eagle pattern. These were obviously added later to attach the wool front piece. The coattail buttons are the standard cavalry ball buttons of the Indian Wars period. The center row of buttons are brown-finished brass with an eagle and "U.S. INDIAN SERVICE" marked on them. These are being made currently for collectors. The buckle is army issue of the Civil War (and later) with eagle and silver wreath. Another type of buckle, round and marked "POLICE," can be seen in figure 24.

Indian Police badges are of two types. One is an American shield with two stars at the top and vertical lines with the words "INDIAN POLICE" in the lower portion. An example of these can be seen in figure 24. The earlier style of badge was the six-pointed type worn by western sheriffs and marshals. There are at least two variations of this kind. The early ones, before about 1891, are engraved with the policeman's name, rank, and agency. The legend on one such badge is "STANDING SOLDIER / LIEUTENANT / U.S. INDIAN / POLICE / Pine Ridge Agency / Dakota." The second style was very similar except that the Indian's name was left off. A typical legend on one of these reads "CAPTAIN / OF / U.S. INDIAN / POLICE / ROSEBUD / S.D." It is probable that badges varied somewhat from agency to agency. One badge, after 1891, had the following legend: "STANDS FIRST / MARSHAL / PINE RIDGE / S.D."

One other badge was worn by Tetons and other Indians. The Miller 101 Ranch issued two types of police badges to employees. The early ones are a circle with piercing to produce a five-pointed star in the center (fig. 195). Figure 196 is Bear

figure 194. Uniform of Indian policeman and scout Fool Bear from Standing Rock Reservation. (KOL)

figure 195. An early Miller's 101 Ranch Show badge. (SI)

Shield, an Oglala, with a regular five-pointed star from the Miller show, the second type of badge.

A crossed-arrows helmet ornament worn by Indian scouts in the United States Army during the late Indian Wars period is illustrated in figure 197. Only little symbols like this remained by 1890 to differentiate the red from white warriors in America.

figure 196. *A later Miller's 101 Ranch Show badge, worn by Bear Shield. (SI)*

figure 197. *Crossed-arrows helmet ornament issued as insignia to Indian scouts by the army in the late Indian Wars period. (MFT)*

Notes

1. Edwin T. Denig, "Indian Tribes of the Upper Missouri," *Forty-sixth Annual Report of the Bureau of American Ethnology, 1928–1929* (Washington: G.P.O., 1930), p. 591.
2. Thompson, *Fort Union Trading Post*, p. 141.
3. Ibid.
4. Interview with John Choloff by John C. Ewers, Pine Ridge, South Dakota, September 25, 1947.
5. Norman Feder, "Plains Indian Metalworking" *American Indian Tradition* 8, no. 2 (1962): 62.
6. Sir Richard Burton, *The Look of the West, 1860*, ed. Robert G. Athearn (Lincoln: University of Nebraska Press, [1963]), p. 70.
7. "Inventory of Stock the Property of Pierre Chouteau Jr. & Co. U.M.O. on Hand at Fort Union 15th May 1851," *Contributions to the Historical Society of Montana* 10 (1940): 210.
8. Matthew C. Field, *Prairie and Mountain Sketches* (Norman: University of Oklahoma Press, 1957), p. 181.
9. Robert Alberts, "Trade Silver and Indian Silver Work in the Great Lakes Region," *Wisconsin Archaeologist* 31, no. 1 (March 1953): 62.
10. Maximilian, *Travels*, pp. 321–22.
11. Reuben Gold Thwaites, ed., *Early Western Travels, 1748–1846* (Cleveland: Arthur H. Clark Co., 1906), vol. 25, pl. 50.
12. Osgood, *Field Notes of Captain William Clark*, p. 235.
13. Claus Papers, vol. IX, pp. 287–90, Manuscript Group 10, Public Archives of Canada, Ottawa, Ontario, Canada.
14. Frederick W. Hodge, *Handbook of American Indians North of Mexico*, Bureau of American Ethnology Bulletin 30 (Washington: G.P.O., 1907), pt. 1, p. 830.
15. Bauman L. Belden, *Indian Peace Medals Issued in the United States* (New York: American Numismatic Society, 1927), p. 26.
16. For detailed information on the descriptions of American medals for Indians, see ibid., pls. 13–32, and Francis Paul Prucha, *Indian Peace Medals in American History* (Madison: State Historical Society of Wisconsin, 1971), pp. 100–134.
17. Thompson, *Fort Union Trading Post*, p. 140.
18. Belden, *Indian Peace Medals*, p. 41.
19. Ibid., p. 42.
20. Ibid.
21. Catlin, *North American Indians*, vol. 1, pl. 99.
22. Indian Office, Finance Division Contracts and Bonds, Supplies, vol. 5, p. 399, July 11, 1878, RG 75, NARS.
23. Thompson, *Fort Union Trading Post*, p. 141; Denig, "Indian Tribes," p. 587.
24. Rosemary Ellison, "Plains Indian Metalwork," *Smoke Signals*, no. 52 (Spring 1967), p. 6.
25. Feder, "Plains Indian Metalworking," 104–5.
26. Mallery, "Pictographs," pl. LXIX.
27. Ibid., pls. LVI, LVII, LVIII.
28. Maximilian, *Travels*, p. 325.
29. Francis Parkman, *The Oregon Trail* (Boston: Ginn and Co., 1910), p. 81.
30. Burton, *Look of the West*, p. 70.
31. Feder, "Plains Indian Metalworking," "List of Hairplates in the Literature," p. 63; "List of Photographs (1868–1912)," p. 70; "Discussion of Surviving Examples," pp. 70–71.
32. Abel, *Tabeau's Narrative*, pp. 176–77.

33. Burton, *Look of the West*, p. 70.
34. Depredation Claim No. 7099, G. P. Beauvais vs. Minniconjou and Northern Cheyenne Indians, Records of the United States Court of Claims, RG 123 and 205, NARS, and "Special Abstracts of Disbursement by John B. Sanborn for Indian Peace Commission Dec. 10, 1868," notation of payment to Poultney and Trimble, New York, April 3, 1868, Records of the General Accounting Office, Washington, D.C.
35. T. L. Green, "A Forgotten Fur Trading Post," *Nebraska History* 15, no. 1 (January–March 1934): 44.
36. "Notes and References," *Contributions to the Historical Society of Montana* 10 (1940): 259.

Selected Bibliography

1. Manuscript Material

General Accounting Office Records, Washington, D.C.
Missouri Historical Society, Saint Louis, Mo.
    Chouteau Accounts
    Chouteau-Maffitt Collections
    Fort Pierre Letterbook
National Archives and Records Service, Washington, D.C.
    RG 75, Records of the Bureau of Indian Affairs
        Finance Division, Contract Books, Office of Indian Affairs
        Office of Indian Affairs, Letters Received
        Upper Platte Agency, Letters Received
    RG 123 and 205, Records of the United States Court of Claims
    Cartographic Section. Lieutenant G. K. Warren's Reconnaissance of the White River, 1854
New-York Historical Society, New York, N.Y.
    American Fur Company's Papers
    Orders Outward
Public Archives of Canada, Ottawa, Ontario
    Manuscript Group 10
    Claus Papers
Miscellaneous Manuscripts
"Army Medical Museum Catalogue," Armed Forces Institute of Pathology Museum, Washington, D.C.

2. Books

Abel, Annie Heloise, ed. *Tabeau's Narrative of Loisel's Expedition to the Upper Missouri*. Norman: University of Oklahoma Press, 1939.

American State Papers. II. Indian Affairs. Washington: G.P.O., 1834.

Annual Report of the Commissioner of Indian Affairs, 1870. Washington: G.P.O., 1871.

Bad Heart Bull, Amos, and Helen H. Blish, *A Pictographic History of the Oglala Sioux*. Lincoln: University of Nebraska Press, 1967.

Belden, Bauman L. *Indian Peace Medals Issued in the United States*. New York: American Numismatic Society, 1927.

Biddle, Nicholas, ed. *History of the Expedition under the Command of Captains Lewis and Clark*. New York: Allerton Book Co., 1922.

Burton, Sir Richard. *The Look of the West, 1860*. Edited by Robert G. Athearn. Lincoln: University of Nebraska Press, [1963].

Carver, Jonathan. *Travels through the Interior Parts of North America*. Minneapolis: Ross and Haines, Inc., 1956.

Catlin, George. *North American Indians*. 2 vols. Philadelphia: Leary, Stuart, and Co., 1913.

Clark, W. P. *The Indian Sign Language*. Philadelphia: L. R.

Hamersly and Co., 1885.

Denig, Edwin T., "Indian Tribes of the Upper Missouri," *Forty-sixth Annual Report of the Bureau of American Ethnology, 1928–1929*, pp. 375–628. Washington: G.P.O., 1930.

Densmore, Frances. *Teton Sioux Music*. Bureau of American Ethnology Bulletin 61. Washington: G.P.O., 1918.

Dodge, Richard. *Our Wild Indians*. Hartford, Conn.: A. D. Worthington and Co., 1883.

Ewers, John C. *Indian Life on the Upper Missouri*. Norman: University of Oklahoma Press, 1968.

Ferris, W. A. *Life in the Rocky Mountains*. Denver: Old West Publishing Co., 1940.

Graham, Col. W. A., ed. *Official Record of the Court of Inquiry concerning the Conduct of Major Marcus A. Reno at the Little Bighorn, June 25–26, 1876*. Pacific Palisades, Calif.: W. A. Graham, 1951.

Hamilton, T. M. *Early Indian Trade Guns*. Lawton, Okla.: Museum of the Great Plains, 1968.

———. *Native American Bows*. York, Pa.: George Shumway, 1972.

Hanson, Charles E., Jr. *The Northwest Gun*. Lincoln: Nebraska State Historical Society, 1955.

———. *The Plains Rifle*. Harrisburg, Pa.: Stackpole Publishing Co., 1960.

Hodge, Frederick W., ed. *Handbook of American Indians North of Mexico*. Bureau of American Ethnology Bulletin 30. Washington: G.P.O., 1907.

Hyde, George E. *Red Cloud's Folk: A History of the Oglala Sioux*. Norman: University of Oklahoma Press, 1937.

———. *Spotted Tail's Folk: A History of the Brule Sioux*. Norman: University of Oklahoma Press, 1961.

Illustrated Catalogue of United States Cartridge Company's Collection of Firearms. Lowell, Mass.: United States Cartridge Co., n.d. [ca. 1903].

Josephy, Alvin M. *The American Heritage Book of Indians*. New York: American Heritage Publishing Co., 1961.

Kappler, Charles, comp. and ed. *Indian Affairs, Laws, and Treaties*. Vol. 2. Washington: G.P.O., 1904.

Kinnaird, Lawrence, ed. *Spain in the Mississippi Valley*. 3 vols. Washington: G.P.O., 1946.

Mallery, Garrick. "Pictographs of the North American Indians." *Fourth Annual Report of the Bureau of American Ethnology, 1882–1883*, pp. 3–256. Washington: G.P.O., 1886.

———. "Picture Writing of the North American Indians." *Tenth Annual Report of the Bureau of American Ethnology, 1888–1889*. Washington: G.P.O., 1893.

Mason, O. T. "North American Bows, Arrows, and Quivers." *Smithsonian Annual Report, 1893*, pp. 631–81. Washington: G.P.O., 1894.

Maximilian, Alexander Phillip, Prince of Wied-Neuwied. *Travels in the Interior of North America*. Vol. 23 of *Early Western Travels, 1748–1846*, edited by Reuben Gold Thwaites. Cleveland: Arthur H. Clark Co., 1906.

Mercer, Henry C. *Ancient Carpenters' Tools*. Doylestown, Pa.: Bucks County Historical Society, 1951.

Osgood, Ernest Staples, ed. *The Field Notes of Captain William Clark, 1803–1805*. New Haven: Yale University Press, 1964.

Parkman, Francis. *The Oregon Trail*. Boston: Ginn and Co., 1910.

Parsons, John, and John DuMont. *Firearms in the Custer Battle*. Harrisburg, Pa.: Telegraph Press, 1953.

Peterson, Harold. *American Indian Tomahawks*. New York: Museum of the American Indian / Heye Foundation, 1965.

Pike, Zebulon. *Sources of the Mississippi and the Western Louisiana Territory*. Ann Arbor, Mich.: University Microfilms, 1966.

Potomac Corral of the Westerners. *Great Western Indian Fights*. New York: Doubleday, 1960. Reprinted Lincoln: University of Nebraska Press, 1966.

Powell, J. W., ed. *Geographic Surveys of the Missouri Basin*. Washington: G.P.O., 1879.

Prucha, Francis Paul. *Indian Peace Medals in American History*. Madison: State Historical Society of Wisconsin, 1971.

Robinson, Doane. *A History of the Dakota or Sioux Indians*. Minneapolis: Ross and Haines, 1955.

Ross, Marvin C. *The West of Alfred Jacob Miller*. Norman: University of Oklahoma Press, 1968.

Russell, Carl P. *Firearms, Traps, and Tools of the Mountain Men*. New York: Alfred A. Knopf, 1967.

Thompson, Erwin N. *Fort Union Trading Post*. Washington: National Park Service, 1968.

Thwaites, Reuben Gold, ed. *Early Western Travels, 1748–1846*. Vol. 25. Cleveland: Arthur H. Clark Co., 1906.

Wissler, Clark. *Indians of the Plains*. New York: American Museum of Natural History, 1948.

3. Periodicals

Alberts, Robert. "Trade Silver and Indian Silver Work in the Great Lakes Region." *Wisconsin Archaeologist* 31, no. 1 (March 1953): 58–70.

Camp, W. M. "Discovery of the Lost Site of the Slim Buttes Battle." *South Dakota Historical Collections* 9 (1918): 55–68.

"A Day at the Birmingham Factories." *Penny Magazine* (London), n.s. 13 (1844): 506–10.

Ellison, Rosemary. "Plains Indian Metalwork." *Smoke Signals*, no. 52 (Spring 1967), pp. 2–20.

Engagés, The. "Indian Awls." *Museum of the Fur Trade Quarterly* 7, no. 2 (Summer 1971): 2–3.

Engagés, The. "Trade Fire Steels." *Museum of the Fur Trade Quarterly* 7, no. 4 (Winter 1971): 2–4.

Feder, Norman. "Plains Indian Metalworking." *American Indian Tradition* 8, no. 2, pt. 1 (March 1962): 55–74; no. 2, pt. 2 (August 1962): 96–112.

Feraca, Stephen E., and James H. Howard. "The Identity and Demography of the Dakota or Sioux Tribe." *Plains Anthropologist* 8, no. 20 (May 1963): 80–85.

Hanson, Charles E., Jr. "Hand Dags." *Museum of the Fur Trade Quarterly* 6, no. 1 (Spring 1970): 2–5.

———. "The Post War Indian Gun Trade." *Museum of the Fur Trade Quarterly* 4, no. 3 (Fall 1968): 1–11.

———. "The St. Louis Shot Tower." *Museum of the Fur Trade Quarterly* 3, no. 3 (Fall 1967: 2–5.

Hanson, James A. "Upper Missouri Arrowheads." *Museum of the Fur Trade Quarterly* 8, no. 4 (Winter 1972): 4–9.

"Inventory of Stock the property of Pierre Chouteau Jr. & Co. U.M.O. on Hand at Fort Benton 4th May 1851," "Inventory of Stock the property of Pierre Chouteau Jr. & Co. U.M.O. on Hand at Fort Union 15th May 1851," and "Notes and References." *Contributions to the Historical Society of Montana* 10 (1940): 201–59.

Metcalf, George. "Two Relics of the Wounded Knee Massacre." *Museum of the Fur Trade Quarterly* 2, no. 4 (Winter 1966): 1–4.

Neuman, Robert W. "Porcupine Quill Flatteners from the Central United States." *American Antiquity* 26, no. 1 (1960): 99–102.

Switzer, Ronald H. "Butcher Knives as Historical Sources." *Museum of the Fur Trade Quarterly* 8, no. 1 (Spring 1972): 5–7.

Thwaites, Reuben Gold, ed. "Memoranda Relative to the Indian Trade." *Collections of the Historical Society of Wisconsin* 12 (1892): 78–82.

———. "1700: Le Sueur's Voyage up the Mississippi." *Collections of the Historical Society of Wisconsin* 16 (1902): 177–93.

Index

American Brass Kettle Manufacturing Co., 59
American Fur Co., 8, 9, 17–18, 31, 50–52, 66
American Horse (Oglala), 71
Ames, O. (spade maker), 67
Annuity goods, government, 9, 18, 21, 26, 53, 57, 59, 65, 70, 90, 99
Arapaho Indians, 4
Arikara Indians, 4, 5, 6, 75
Arm bands, 75, 76, 83–84
Army, United States, 10
Army Medical Museum, 33
Arrowheads, 13, 26–31, 60; collected by Catlin, 28; hunting, 26; Indian Wars, 28; target or field, 31; war, 26–27
Assiniboin Indians, 4
"Assiniboin" lances, 31–33
Astor, John Jacob, 8, 16, 18, 87
Awl cases, 105–6
Awls, 13, 61–62
Axes, 13, 54–56

Badges, 106–7
Bad Heart Bull, Amos (Oglala), 45
Ball clubs, 11
Barnett (Northwest fun maker), 16, 17, 18–19
Beads, brass, 79–80, 106; cut steel, 79–80
Bear Shield (Oglala), 106–7, 108
Beauvais, G. P. (trader), 68, 99
Belden, Bauman (author), 88
Belgian Northwest guns, 16, 18–19, 64
Bells, 37, 80–82; hawk, 80
Belt disks, 75, 96–97
Belt drops, 96–97
Bent and St. Vrain, 8
Bertrand (steamboat), 53
Big Soldier (Brule), 39
Bits, Mexican, 68–69
Black Bear (Oglala), 92
Black Elk (Oglala), 26, 80
Black Elk, Ben (Oglala), 26
Blackfoot Indians, 9
Blackfoot Sioux (Sia Sapa) Indians, 4, 26
Black Horn (Hunkpapa), 44, 45
Blades for ball clubs, 11

Blood, I. (edged-tool maker), 55, 56
Bodmr, Karl (artist), 35, 85
Bordeaux, James (trader), 55
Bracelets, 75, 76, 84
Breast plate, German silver, 105
Breechloading firearms, 22–24
Bridles, German silver mounted, 106
Brotherton, Lieutenant Colonel D. H., 36, 53
Brule Indians, 4, 15, 24, 26, 57, 75, 76
Buckles, 106
Bullhead, Lieutenant, 101, 103
Burnette (Northwest gun), 16, 18–19
Burton, Sir Richard (traveler), 78, 93, 99
Buttons, 104, 106–7

Calumet, steel, 13
Camp, W. M., 71
Campbell, Robert (trader and agent), 8
Canadian traders, 5

Carver, Jonathan (traveler), 10, 49
Catlin, George (artist), 27–29, 31–35, 49–50
Census roster, Oglala, 92
Chain, brass, 79, 92, 98
Chance, W. and Son (gun makers), 17–18
Cheyenne Indians, 4, 20, 72
Chippewa Indians, 3, 4, 7, 9, 57
Choloff, John (storekeeper), 77
Chouteau, Pierre, Jr. *See* Pierre Chouteau, Jr., and Co.
Civil War, 9, 21, 23–24, 35, 45, 57, 64, 75, 96, 98
Clark, W. P. (scout), 26, 27, 29
Clark, William (explorer), 6, 9, 14–15, 17, 26, 40, 42, 61, 77, 104
Clement & Maynard (hoe makers), 67
Clubs, 11, 35–38
Coats, 6
Coffee pots, 60
Collins (ax maker), 56, 57
Colt revolvers, 24, 26

115

Columbia Fur Co., 8
Comanche Indians, 90
Conches. *See* Belt disks *and* Belt drops
Cooking utensils, 57–60
Cree Indians, 3–4
Crosses, 75, 92–93, 101–3
Crow Agency (Montana), 20
Crucifixes, Catholic, 100–103
Cups, tin, 60
Cutler, Hiram (cutler), 50–51, 68

Dag knives, 9, 33
Dakota, 6
Dangles, 77
David, Lucas (trader), 6
De Girardin, E. (traveler), 14
D'Eglise, Jacques (trader), 7
Denig, Edwin T. (trader), 75, 90
De Smet, Father Pierre-Jean, 101, 104
Dodd, Frank, 30
Dodge, Richard Irving (army officer), 38
Durfee and Peck, 9

Earbobs, 75–77
Earrings, brass wire, 43, 92, 99
Ear wheels, 75, 76
Eastman, Seth (artist), 56
Elk (Oglala), 80
Ellison, Rosemary, 90
Enfield muskets, 22
English, 3, 6
Ewers, John C., 4

Feder, Norman, 78, 93
Ferris, W. A. (mountain man), 45
Field, Matthew (traveler), 83
Files, 70
Firearms, 6–7, 10–12, 14–26
Firesteels, 13, 68
Flags, 6
Fleshing tools, 63–64
Fool Bear (Hunkpapa), 106, 107
Fort Buford (North Dakota), 20
Fort John (Wyoming and Nebraska), 8. *See also* Fort Laramie
Fort Keogh (Montana), 64
Fort Laramie (Wyoming), 8, 18, 33, 78, 83, 93, 94
Fort Pierre (South Dakota), 8, 14, 18
Fort Robinson (Nebraska), 23, 26, 51, 57–58, 104
Forts, established by traders, 8
Fort Union (North Dakota), 8, 49, 75, 80, 90
Fort Yates (North Dakota), 64, 101, 103
Fox (cutlery), 38
Fox, Livingston & Co., 8
French, 3, 6
French and Indian War, 13
Frontenac, Comte Louis de Buade de (governor of New France), 5
Frost, S. A., and Son (ornament makers), 77
Furnas, Governor R. W., 35
Furnis (cutler), 50, 51

Gardiner, William (photographer), 93
German silver, 75, 78, 83, 84, 91–93, 96
Ghost Dance, 72
Golcher, J. (gun maker), 20
Good Buffalo (Oglala), 91
Good Voiced Crow (Teton), 44, 45
Gorgets, 75, 76, 90
Great Lakes traders, 5
Greaves (cutler), 51
Grills, cooking, 60
Gunstock clubs, 35

Hairplates, 93–96; miniature, 93–95
Hamilton, J. A. (trader), 58
Hamilton, T. M., 12
Hanson, Charles E., Jr., 16, 88–90, 96–97
Hatchets, 56–57, 96
Hawken, S. (gun maker), 20
Hazen, Mrs. M. M., 57
Headbands (hat crowns), 75, 76
Heart River, 4
Helmet ornament, Indian Scout, 107
Hené, Hugh (trader), 6
Hennepin, Father Louis, 3
Henry (repeating rifle), 22
Henry, J. (gun maker), 19–20
Hide scrapers, 62–64; Cheyenne, 62; bits or blades, 63
Hoes, 67
Hoff, Colonel John Rensellaer, 38
Horse equipment, 68–70

Horstmann, G. (button maker), 104
Hudson, Bill, 30
Hudson's Bay, 3, 6
Hudson's Bay Co., 6, 9, 18, 20, 33, 38, 68
Huffman, L. A. (photographer), 37
Hunkpapa Sioux Indians, 4

Indian Affairs, Bureau of, 10
Indian Police, 22; uniforms, 106–7
Interior, Department of, 22
Iron Crow (Oglala), 92
Iron Hawk (Oglala), 92

Jacot, W. (Northwest gun supplier), 16, 17
James River, 5
Jerome, Father, 103

Kettles, 12–13, 57–59
Kiowa Indians, 4, 9, 90
Knife clubs, 11, 35–38
Knives, 49–54, 71–72; bowie, 37, 54; early, 11, 13; Green River, *see* Russell, J., and Co.

Lacy (gun maker), 18
Lamson and Goodnow Manufacturing Co. (cutlery), 38, 53–54
Lance heads, 13, 31–35
Lead, 84
Leatherworking tools, 60
Leman, Henry (gun maker), 17–18, 20–21

Le Sueur, Pierre Charles (entrepreneur), 3, 5–6, 11, 14
Lewis, Meriwether (explorer), 6, 9, 14–15, 17, 26, 42, 61, 77, 104
Lisa, Manuel (trader), 8
Little Big Horn, Battle of the (Custer Battle), 20–21, 23, 26, 29, 69
Little Hawk (Oglala), 92
Loisel, Regis (trader), 6
Long Dog (Oglala), 92, 101–2
Louisiana, 7
Low Dog (Oglala), 40
Lupton, Lancaster (trader), 8
Lyons, Ray (reservation trader), 97

Mackinac Island, 6, 7, 15, 85
Malgares, Lieutenant Don Facundo, 86
Malliet (militia officer), 6
Mandan Indians, 4, 6, 14, 104
Manhattan Cutlery Company, 37
Matches, sulfur, 68
Maximilian, Prince (traveler), 35, 57, 61–62, 64, 84–85, 93
Mdewakanton Sioux Indians, 3
Medals, 6, 13, 85–90; Catholic, Immaculate Conception, 100; "miraculous," 104. *See also* Peace Medals
Menominee Indians, 83
Metal, importance of to Tetons, xiii
Metcalf, Dr. George, 26

Métis (Canadian half-bloods), 20
Mexican, bridles, 106; silversmiths, 90
Miller, Alfred Jacob (artist), 31, 32, 93–94
Miller's 101 Wild West Show, medals, 90; badges, 106–7
Miniconjou Sioux Indians, 4, 26, 90, 99
Minnesota, 5, 7; River, 3; Massacre, 36
Mississippi River, 3, 6
Mississippi traders, 5
Missouri Fur Company, 8
Missouri River, 3, 4, 6, 33
Missouri war ax, 42
Michilimackinac Company, 8
Murphy, H. (arrowhead maker), 26
Museum of the American Indians, 37, 106
Museum of the Fur Trade, 18, 30

Nebraska State Historical Society, 86
Needles, 65–66
Neuman, Robert W., 67
Nickel silver. *See* German silver
Niobrara cross, 97
Niobrara River, 50
No Flesh (Oglala), 92
Northwest Co., 6, 7, 33
Northwestern Fur Co., 9
Northwest guns, 12, 15–20

Oglala Sioux Indians, 4, 24, 26

One Knife (Hunkpapa), 36
Ordnance Bureau, United States, 54
Ordway, Sergeant (explorer), 15, 45
Oregon Trail, 61
Ornaments, metal, 13, 75–110
Otis, Forest (storekeeper), 63

Parkman, Francis (traveler), 93
Pawnee Indians, 4, 88
Pawnee Killer (Oglala), 98, 99
Peace medals, government, 85–87; trader's, 87–90
Pectorals, 9, 75, 90, 92
Pierre Chouteau, Jr., and Co., 8, 9, 18, 20, 52, 57–58, 60, 87
Pike, Zebulon Montgomery (explorer), 7, 15
Pine Ridge Agency (South Dakota), 72, 77
Pipes, lead-inlaid, 85
Pistols, 24–26
Platte River, 4, 8, 80
Poplar River (Montana), 92
Poultney and Trimble (annuity contractors), 59
Prairie du Chien (Wisconsin), 86
Pratte, Chouteau and Co., 8

Quill flatteners, 66–67

Red Cloud (Oglala), 39
Red Dog (Oglala), 24
Religious objects, 100–104
Remington revolvers, 22–26

Reno, Major Marcus, 22
Republican River, 30
Revolutionary War, 6
Rifles, trade, 20–21
Rings, 75, 77–78, 98; iron, for saddles, 70
Risley, D. R. (Indian agent), 60
Rodgers (arrowhead maker), 26
Running Water (Teton), 94
Russell, Carl P., 68
Russell, J., and Co. (cutlers), 26, 37, 50–52

Saddles, McClellan, 25, 69–70
Saint Louis, 6, 7, 8, 58
St. Peters Indian Agency (Minnesota), 14, 40
Sans Arc (Itazipco) Sioux Indians, 4, 26, 42–43, 101
Santa Fe, 86
Santee Division of Sioux Indians, 3
Saone tribes of Tetons, 4, 33
Sargant (Belgian gun mark), 18
Scissors, 65
Scythe blades, 64
Sewing tools, 61–62, 65–66
Sharps rifles, 23, 24
Shoshoni Indians, 4
Shotguns, 26
Sisseton Sioux Indians, 3, 7
Sitting Bull (Hunkpapa), 20–22, 54, 101–2
Sitting Bull the minor (Oglala), 36
Skillets, 59–60

117

Slim Buttes, Battle of (South Dakota), 71
Smith and Wesson revolvers, 26
Smithsonian Institution, 20, 26, 28, 29, 33–35, 37, 38, 40, 53, 54, 57, 64, 69, 78, 84, 92
Southwest Co., 8
Spades, 67
Spanish, 5, 6, 7
Spencer (repeating rifle), 22
Spoons, 72
Spotted Eagle (Teton), 37
Springfield carbines, 23
Stabbed Plenty (Teton), 37
Standing Rock Agency (North Dakota), 22, 38, 62, 66, 72, 106
Standing Soldier (Oglala), 106
Standish, Miles (blacksmith), 31
Stands First (Oglala), 106
Swords, 45–47; Spanish blade, 31

Tabeau, Pierre Antoine (trader), 5–7, 24, 31, 49, 98
Tacks, brass, 40, 50, 90
Tanning tools, 62–64
Taylor, Henry H., and Brother (cutlers), 36
Teakettles, iron, 71
Teton Division of Sioux Indians, 3–7, 9
Teton National Park Museum, 51
Thigh (Oglala), 91
Tomahawks, 38–43, 98
Tools, metal, 49–74; miscellaneous, 70–72
Trade, buffalo robe, 7; historic centers of, 10; demise of, 10; mountain man, 7; prehistoric, 4; prohibitions on, 10; protohistoric, 4–5
Trade goods, early, 11–13
Trade guns. *See* Northwest guns
Traps, beaver, 60

Tryon, E. K. (gun maker), 19–21, 64
Two Kettle (Ooenonpa) Sioux Indians, 4, 26

Uniforms, Indian Police, 106, 107
Upper Missouri Outfit, 8
Upper Platte Agency (Wyoming), 59

Wahpekute Sioux Indians, 3
Wahpeton Sioux Indians, 3
Ward, J. (cutler), 26, 51, 52
War of 1812, 6, 8
Warren, Lieutenant G. K. (explorer), 88
Weapons, metal, 14–48
Wetmore, Colonel William Boerum, 31
Whetstone Agency (Nebraska), 60
White Eyes (Oglala), 91
White Stone Hill, Battle of (North Dakota), 33

White Thunder (Brule), 105
Whitney-Kennedy rifle, 22
Wiciyela Division of Sioux Indians, 3
Wilson, John (Cutler), 52
Winchester repeating rifle, 21–22
Winter Counts, Teton, 6, 14, 42
Wire, brass, 13, 84, 92, 98–100; iron, 100
Wounded Knee, Battle of (South Dakota), 38, 52, 65, 71–72, 75, 77, 97–99
Wrist bands. *See* Bracelets
Wyoming, University of, Anthropology Collections, 40

Yankton Sioux Indians, 3, 6, 7, 15, 33, 35
Yanktonai Sioux Indians, 3
Yellowstone River, 20
Ylinueses (Spanish district), 6
Young-Man-Afraid-of-His-Horse (Oglala), 23, 78, 92, 98

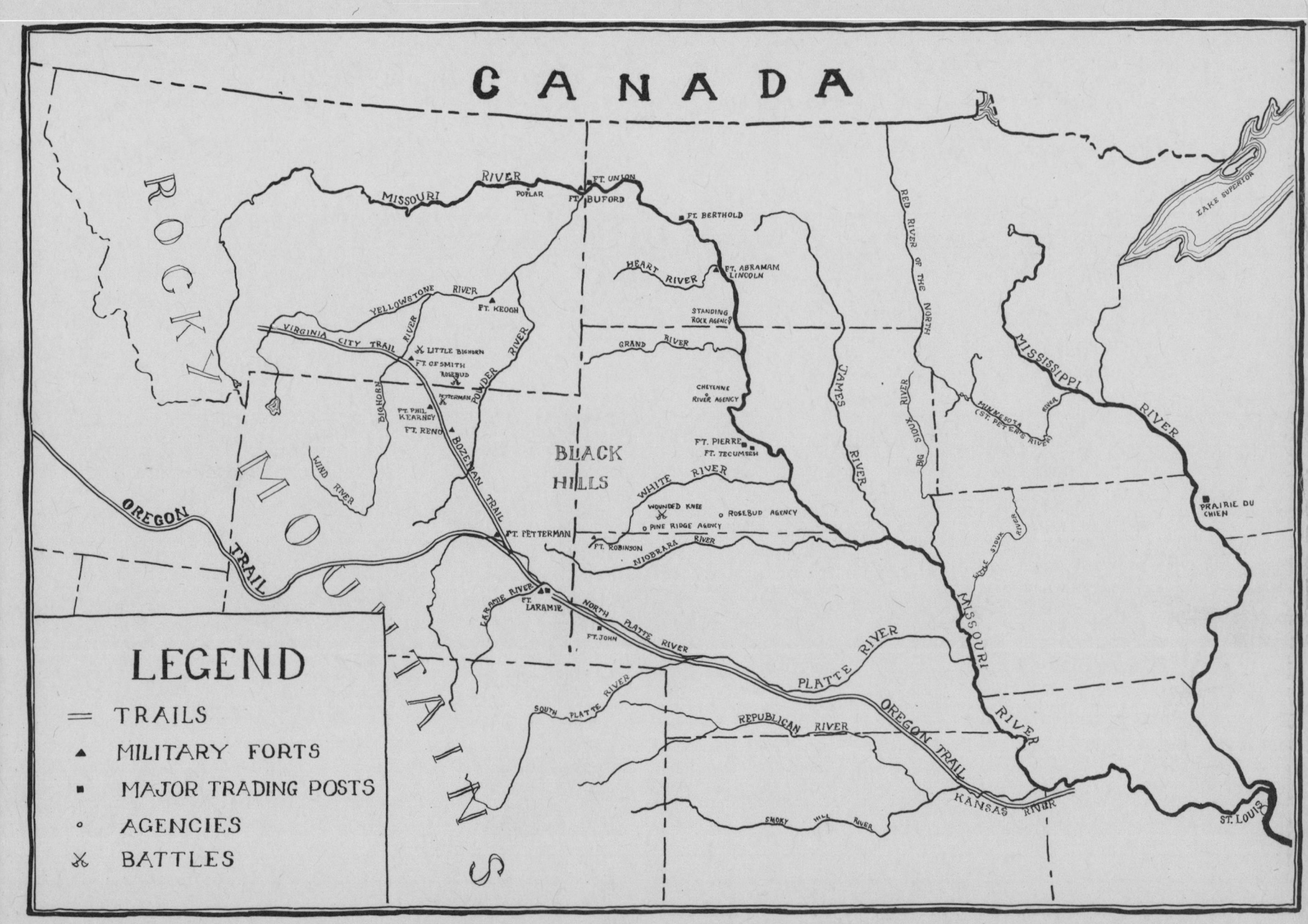